FARANJI

FARANJI

A Venture into Ethiopia

To Julia & Bob —
These farmers are
for comparison —
or not? with
Eastern Washington
farmers. Judy

JUDITH REYNOLDS BROWN

With photographs by the author
and portraits by Noel Benson

FITHIAN PRESS
SANTA BARBARA • 1994

For Asellefech—I needed her, she wanted me.

Copyright ©1994 by Judith Reynolds Brown
Printed in the United States of America

Design and typography by Jim Cook

Published by Fithian Press
A division of Daniel & Daniel, Publishers, Inc.
P.O. Box 1525
Santa Barbara, California 93102

LIBRARY OF CONGRESS CATALOGING-IN-PUBLICATION DATA
Brown, Judith Reynolds
    Faranji: a venture into Ethiopia / Judith Reynolds Brown.
        p. cm.
    ISBN 1-56474-072-2
    1. Godino (Ethiopia)—Description and travel. 2. Economic
assistance—Ethiopia—Godino. 3. Brown, Judith Reynolds, —
Journeys—Ethiopia—Godino. 4. Brown, Jack—Journeys—
Ethiopia—Godino. I. Title.
DT390.G63B76   1994
916.3'3—dc20   93-11475
                                                       CIP

Contents

Photo section follows page 120

1.
A Dialogue with Myself

THIS venture began when I knew nothing about Ethiopia, except that it had lately been hit by civil war, drought, and famine. I arrived in the country innocent about how much any organization or individual might accomplish in a third-world country, but determined to see. I left the country fiercely loyal to a group of Ethiopians I had come to care about, and naïvely unaware of the forces that would emerge to gnaw away at the development efforts our small group had managed to start.

For my husband, Jack, and I, Ethiopia began in the Addis Ababa airport reception lounge. It started when neither of us had a visitor's entry visa and were consequently stalled on a worn vinyl loveseat with shiny pipe arms. Without visas, the Ethiopian authorities would not let us in.

Sitting in that bare, high-ceilinged airport lounge, I began to ask the questions I should have asked before I left home.

"Why Ethiopia?" my practical self asked.

"Because it's the third world," my adventuresome self said.

"But there's a war on here, and drought," my practical self whined. "Do you really want to see people starve? You could get caught in the crossfire."

"That's sheer drama! We're not going to the war zone," my adventurous side countered.

"But your visa didn't arrive, and the people you've agreed to work with are hopelessly disorganized, or they would have met you," the voice of practicality grumbled.

"Would you rather travel as a tourist?"

"Never! It's always better to settle, to work as you travel. And what's more, this time we get to try working as a team with Soviets!"

"But are you really going to make it to the village?"

"We better! We didn't come here to stay in a city!"

"But without language, you'll never get a real sense of the people!"

"We're already here. It's too late for doubts. I'm no longer snugly ensconced on our home's lush green island, and if this venture turns to misadventure, I'll have no one but my too-impulsive self to blame!"

The tone of my own resolve jolted me back to the airport sofa. I stared out at the low customs counter on the other side of the huge room. I had expected the exotic. This was merely shabby. After rushing about the world, too full of our own motion to take time to question, we had been brought to a full stop. Stalled in a most unlikely spot. The future boded neither ill nor good—it didn't bode at all!

Strange airports, languages, and the odd ways other nations run themselves were not new to my husband and me. Before we were married in our early twenties, we had each separately spent more than a year in Quaker work-camps in Europe. Thirty-eight years ago we had married with an agreement to work in as much of the world as we could. We'd spent six years in Gaziantep, in the remote eastern part of Turkey, from 1957 to 1962 and again in 1970 and 1971. There Jack practiced general medicine in a fifty-bed mission hospital. Later, in 1981, we spent six months in New Zealand and six months in Australia while Jack taught psychiatry at medical schools in Dunedin and Newcastle.

The current trip was a post-retirement foray. Jack had retired and we had left for a continuation of our old commitment. We had just finished a four-month stint in Edinburgh,

Scotland, where Jack worked part-time as a volunteer in a psychiatric program. Edinburgh was to have been the cultural and contrasting preparation for Ethiopia. But Jack's general medicine was rusty, and in third-world countries psychiatry seems an esoteric and culture-bound skill, so he was determined this time to do something other than medicine.

Now, in January 1991, we were eager to go deeper than what we'd read about Ethiopia and to experience it for ourselves. But where were our hosts? We hadn't expected to be met and carried off on an elephant! But we had expected to be met.

"You were warned that the Ethiopian government allows no visitors whom they did not invite, but you thought you had an invitation," I reminded myself.

When we applied to come here with the Seattle branch of Ploughshares, an organization of former Peace Corps members, we were assured they had made an agreement with a group called the Family Service Organization. FSO's purpose was to help the Ethiopian poor to become more self-reliant. It was new and untried, but what could be better? We would work under the Ethiopians themselves, help do what they thought was important, instead of going in like ugly Americans and pushing indigenous people around.

What did we really know about this organization that was to have obtained our visas and met us with our instructions? The arrangements we had made had been casual. We had arrived in Ethiopia fresh from country-hopping around Europe. We had hardly stayed in one place long enough to receive the entry visas they said would be mailed to us.

"If you don't have visas," we were told, "someone will meet you at the airport with them."

But what someone?

Doubts were mushrooming after an interminable wait on these plastic cushions. When we made our plans, our feet, I decided, had been firmly planted in the clouds!

Our flight from London on Ethiopian Airlines had been

unexpectedly comfortable. Due to an airline snafu, we had been bumped to business class from economy and had imbibed that luxury with all the hunger of people indulging their last chance. We touched down at 7:15 A.M., half an hour ahead of schedule. My "wilt" began as I crossed the hot airport tarmac in the blazing heat of that January morning to reach the passport window. When the woman who checked the documents discovered we had no visas, she pointed to this worn sofa. "Wait there," she told us.

I recalled someone saying that if we didn't have a visa we should leave our passports at the airport and proceed into town. But where in town? We knew nothing about how to get there, or even how to get out of this reception lounge.

We were *faranji,* "white foreigners." My Scottish designer wool cardigan and navy blue wool slacks were melting me into a soggy matron. Jack usually looked distinguished—he was tall and curly-gray haired—but now his crumpled corduroy jacket made him look dumpy. How much more "out of place" could we be?

We had nothing to give us prestige. Had we been journalists, our newspaper connections might have whisked us through. But no media had sent us, nor had the U.S. government. Ethiopia had expelled all the Americans it could when its Marxist government came to power in 1974. Addis Ababa was the base for numerous U.N. agency personnel, but we had no such "important" assignment. All we had was a vague sense of clinging piggyback to an Ethiopian agency that hadn't shown up.

For affirmation, I reviewed what I knew. An uncertain number of Ethiopians would be joining four Soviets and four U.S. volunteers to do agricultural work in a village named Godino. I had told my friends playfully that I was going to Africa to dig ditches. We were to be part of a team being sent to work from January to March in an area south of Addis Ababa. The work would introduce new vegetables and organic agricultural methods, and if that took digging ditches, I would dig them.

We would live in tents for three months. Family Service Organization had supposedly established a tent camp at Godino, and would direct our work.

Since it was unthinkable to work on our own in Africa, Ploughshares had found Family Service Organization already working on agricultural development and willing to have us join them. We had paid our airfare and a small amount for room and board, and we were to receive a stipend for spending money while we worked. We had claimed to know little about organic agriculture, but Ploughshares said it didn't matter. The agricultural knowledge we needed would be in the heads of the Ethiopians who sponsored the project; they spoke English and would teach us. We would work under the Ethiopians and live as they lived. We would eat the food provided by an indigenous organization. Our purpose was to model the agricultural methods recommended by FSO to help Ethiopians become healthier and more self-reliant.

Since I had always considered Soviet women tough, I had been mildly unnerved to find that the Soviets who toured the area prior to launching the project had decided to send no women on their team. The camp was too primitive for women. But as a younger woman in Quaker workcamps, I had lived in "tough" settings. Didn't I want to try out my toughness as an older woman? Couldn't almost anything be endured for three short months? Surely the FSO would set up a tolerable volunteer work situation.

I relaxed and for the first time glanced about the airport. We sat in a square cluster of vinyl seats outside the open door of an office that must have had something to do with passports. A few latecomers still straggled out behind the passport booth. A sprinkling of people were still huddled over their bags across the room at customs. Ethiopians whom I guessed must be officials shuffled aimlessly past us. Each of them had fine, straight features and smooth, brown skin. Not one woman had a prominent nose, not a man had grizzled whiskers—they were a handsome lot. The women wore high heels and skirts in casual, western, summer fashion. The men wore shirt sleeves. Persons we guessed were airport staff kept meeting friends and kissing them three times on alternate cheeks ritualistically, without emotion. No one appeared to be either busy or in charge.

Still, we waited. No Ethiopian shared our anxiety. I pulled out a picture from a publicity blurb and stared at Roba Mieso, the Ethiopian executive director of FSO. Eventually he'd surely come to meet us, and I wanted to recognize him. He looked young, but guessing the age of Africans was risky.

Some minutes later I saw the bald head of a tall white man on the far side of the room. He seemed to be looking for someone. Could it be us? We signaled. He saw us and beckoned. The man was Fred Bauman, a Ploughshares volunteer on the previous October-through-December team. He indicated that Roba, the FSO director, with his black skin, could not bluff his way through the security guards into this inner sanctum of the airport.

"Leave your passports, get a receipt for them, and go through customs," he told us.

To hear unaccented English, to receive decisive instructions revived us. We soon followed Fred out of the lounge and past the huge crowd straining against the ropes waiting to greet incoming passengers.

Fred, we learned, had grown restless as a middle-aged apple farmer and had decided to use his skills "to see what Christianity really meant." After volunteering with Habitat for Humanity and building several homes in the Yakima Valley near his Washington state home, he and his wife, Pam, were in their second year of volunteering abroad. He had been able to slip through the airport gate because he had a natural forcefulness and because he'd already spent three months accustoming himself to languageless ways of working in Ethiopia.

Roba, a slight thirty-year-old man with a receding hairline, waited for us in a van in the tree-dotted parking lot. He was of the Oromo tribe. He greeted us in fluent English, as if he already knew us well. His friendly, casual manner was what I had expected, but what startled me was that he felt no need to explain the delay.

A driver named Abebe and a man of uncertain function named Gitachew also waited in the van. We had been moving only about three minutes before we learned that Abebe, the handsome twenty-nine-year-old driver, had five children and another on the way. His English was less facile, but he spoke enough to show us he was a happy-go-lucky, optimistic, gentle-tempered family man. Later we learned that it was Abebe's mechanical genius that kept the old, weary van running.

The morning heat seemed not to have touched Gitachew. His dark glen-plaid summer sport coat looked as if it had just come from the cleaners. He sat facing us, his huge frame folded onto a low stool in the back of the junky van. He was our teammate, the camp buyer. That morning he became the teller of tales. He spoke excellent English, took a clear pride in his country's story, and had many stories to tell of Addis Ababa's history (he explained that the name meant "new flower").

At first I was too busy looking to listen as we pulled out of the parking lot onto the roadway. The roads had wide, dusty shoulders flanking the pot-holed blacktop. I was used to roads intended for vehicles; Addis's roads are as much for feet as for wheels. Our van lumbered along through a parade of Ethiopian people and animals: slender men and women, pot-bellied children, bearded old men, donkeys, goats, all moving slowly in the hot sun. A few were in snappy western dress—sport shirts and bright-colored dresses. Most people wore worn, ill-fitting clothing of colors that had once been bright. Most women wore head scarves, frequently of coarse black netting. Many adults wore gaudy sandals or slippers of colored plastic; the children were barefoot. Women caught my eye who had draped white gauze-like cotton shawls over their heads. The men draped themselves in shawls less often than the women, but white gave those who wore it an added dignity.

At one place, Abebe was forced to stop for a man and his donkey, and Gitachew told us a tale. "Once upon a time a donkey, a dog, and a goat took a ride together on an Ethiopian bus. When they got off, the driver asked each animal for half a *birr*. The donkey paid and left the bus. The goat left the bus and ran off without paying. The dog gave the driver one birr and asked for change, but the driver went off without giving him his change. That is why, when a vehicle comes up behind a goat, he runs off, afraid he'll be caught and have to pay up. The dog chases any vehicle he meets, hoping for the return of his change. The donkey moves aside for nothing! He knows he's paid his fare."

At the time Gitachew told that tale, I didn't know how typical of Ethiopia it was. Dogs, donkeys, and goats are everywhere in that country, and a preoccupation with getting somewhere and what it costs seems ingrained in the Ethiopian psyche.

Regardless of the fact that Addis was on a plateau some 6,000 feet high, the heat pressed in as the van moved slowly. When I removed my sweater, moisture glued my blouse to the vinyl of the van's seat. The breeze from the open window was too weak to chase the flies away from my face. That first morning, I experimented with a gesture that would become a habit: if I thrust my lower lip forward and blew up toward my nose and eyes, I could scatter the flies with the force of my breath.

As we approached the city center, we saw newer four- and five-story cement buildings that seemed to lean on the small corrugated-iron shanties surrounding them. Several ten-story hotels spiked over the other buildings, but nothing overwhelmed as did the myriad storefront shacks angling across each other. The occasional vacant lot teemed with refuse—old rags, paper scraps, orange peels—and the smell of rotting garbage wafted through the van's windows. Walled courtyards lined many of the streets, suggesting that better buildings lurked behind, but the visible structures were mostly rusted and tumble-down. We passed a few public buildings with patches of trim gardens and flowers—showplaces in the midst of seedy chaos. The city was both shabby and smelly.

As we drove through the central streets of Addis, Gitachew grew more voluble about history. He ignored the present to stress Ethiopia's debt to Emperor Haile Selassie's fifty-eight-year reign, which ended in 1974. He boasted that whatever progress Ethiopians have made has come without being colonized by a European nation. Italy occupied Ethiopia for only a short time before the African nation threw the European nation out. As he spoke, Gitachew's veneration of Haile Selassie for his attempts to modernize Ethiopian was clear. Of all the things he said, however, I retained only one detail: before Haile Selassie changed things, bars of salt were used as currency in Ethiopia.

Gitachew had just pointed out Menelik's Palace, Haile Selassie's official residence, when Fred turned from the van's front seat. "The Soviets on our team sort of run things while we're in Addis," he said.

I wondered what that meant, but I said, "I see."

"The Soviet Peace Fund [the Soviet counterpart to Ploughshares in sponsoring our project] has strong ties with Blacha Hospital," he continued. "It's Soviet-run, so we'll be staying on the hospital's top floor for two days before we head for the village."

"I see," I said again.

"We've learned what 'Soviet influence' means," Fred went on. "This country is crawling with Soviets—air force personnel, doctors. . . . We went to a party with the general who commands the air force here. He was eager, friendly. . . ."

"I see," I said yet again, wondering if that was a friendship our new team would choose to cultivate. But we were at the hospital gate, which a guard opened.

We passed into another world inside Balcha Hospital's walled courtyard, where there were several large four-story buildings. Fred told us there were fifty Soviet doctors on the hospital staff. Suddenly we saw flowers blooming in weed-strewn beds, and we were shaded by green trees. There were even scattered areas where the overgrown grass was clipped.

"Ethiopians assume that any white face is a Soviet," Roba said flatly.

"Since 1974, when Mengistu began to consolidate his power, we have seen many Soviet military advisers and other personnel, and European and U.S. influences like the Peace Corps have been pushed out," Gitachew added.

As we approached the hospital's door, our Ethiopian companions became subdued. Did I detect a certain preju-dice against the godless Soviet influence in their country? And was this attitude typical, or was it more pronounced because these Ethiopians were Evangelical Protestants? (Their speech was peppered with words like "blessing," "God willing," and "Alleluia.")

Gitachew had claimed that half of all Ethiopians were Coptic Christians, and 10 percent were Muslims. We guessed that our teammates, being Protestants, were members of a religious minority whose main western contacts had been missionaries. These Ethiopians had known their American Christian benefactors as aides and advocates in procuring education and opportunity, rather than as interlopers.

I felt relieved as I climbed from the van in the green Balcha courtyard. In flying off to Ethiopia we had thought we were flying to oblivion. But Ethiopian was not oblivion. It was a land full of clutter and faded color, and we had been dropped in one of its green spots. We were in for a melting pot of sensation: new people, new geography. That first day we had no inkling of the somber mood in which we would leave the country.

2.
First Impressions—
They're Made to Be Changed

THE van dropped us inside the hospital courtyard, and our Ethiopian colleagues drove off. Roba seemed unassuming for the director of an energetic effort, but I sensed we were yet to experience his dedication. Abebe's cheer had been a good antidote to the gloom of our airport wait, and Gitachew's stories had filled us in on what Ethiopians were proud of in their heritage. Although only Gitachew was going to be with us consistently at camp, these three Ethiopians boded well for the others we might know in camp life. Now it was the Soviets we wondered about!

We entered Balcha hospital, and Fred, his gaunt face shiny as the apples he grew, led us, dragging our luggage up to our temporary dormitory on the third floor. The speckled cement floors were being wet-mopped, but the hospital atmosphere itself made us want to tiptoe along the wide, dark halls. A bright white cotton shawl over her head dignified the woman swishing the mop. Family members stood in uncertain clusters at the doors of patients' rooms. Were they watching these odd foreigners, or were their fixed stares a result of numb worry about their relatives? In a hospital, who does not feel out of place? Would the third floor be different?

We reached the top of a broad cement staircase, and our fellow teammates rushed from their rooms to greet us. Fatigue blurred my first impressions of those four Soviets and two other Americans, but immediately I saw that lack of language would be the real barrier to deriving a sense of the Soviets. I was awed to meet the people with whom I would work closely in the next three months. What if they were impossible? How do you work closely with people with whom you have few ways to communicate? Ruslan, a thirty-eight-year-old Soviet doctor, didn't appear to be "my type." Short, stocky, with a firm presence despite his lack of English, he had sandy, tightly curled red hair and wore a tee-shirt pulled taut across his weight-lifter's chest. Sergei, bristling with twenty-six-year-old bravado, seemed young and glib. Vladislov, a retiring twenty-one-year-old, was hesitant to speak in English but seemed eager to behave in a gentlemanly way. For none of them did I get a strong feeling one way or the other.

One pleasant surprise was that there was a Soviet woman on the team! Clearly, the Soviet Peace Fund had changed its original judgment that the camp was too rough for women and had sent a woman for this second team! Olga was pretty, blond, and slight, looking younger than her thirty-one years. Carefully made up with heavy eye-liner, she tried a few formal English words.

Pam Bauman cocked her wavy-haired, prematurely gray head and took me in with wide eyes and a hug. She had remained in Ethiopia with her husband, Fred, to handle the orientation and transition between our team and the previous Soviet–U.S. team, which had been working in Godino from October to late December. Seeing Pam's impeccable grooming, hearing her melodious voice, I wondered how anyone could be so pert and eager in this dreary setting. At ten in the morning I was already tired.

The only other U.S. volunteer was Ann, a tall, lithe woman of twenty-five, wearing the pants and loose tee-shirt that were her uniform. With thick blond hair and a thin face bearing no scrap of make-up, her strong features were as lovely as if some artist had painted them. I noticed she'd been translating everything, even our banter, for the Soviets. Compared to Pam, Ann seemed boyish.

We were the last foreigners to arrive. The team members were strangers still, but we would know each other well by the time we had worked together for three months. Was it due to our age that our teammates seemed to show a certain deference to Jack and me? I wanted to think that Jack's curly gray hair and cordial manner and my empathetic energy belied our respective sixty-four and sixty years, but I could not tell how they saw us.

The room they ushered us into was painted sick-green. Lined up on opposite walls were two narrow iron beds. In that heat, I looked skeptically at the red woolen blankets with their spotless unbleached muslin covers, but was told that by evening I would want the blankets for warmth. A bare light bulb hung down from the high ceiling. The room's private bath had a toilet which flushed only when you reached into the top of the tank to fiddle with its plumbing. In a corner of the room was an ancient refrigerator which didn't appear to be working.

Since Balcha was a Soviet-run hospital, during our stay there the Soviets, particularly Ruslan, tended to act as hosts to us U.S. volunteers. For our first lunch together, we gathered in the large corner room, which the three Soviet men occupied. We spread the food out on two end-to-end coffee tables. The Americans perched on one of the beds while the Soviets drew up chairs on the other side of the tables. I wondered if this lining up on sides opposite each other would continue through camp meals.

A watery vegetable soup made the first course. Then came bread and a plate with a huge collapsed mound of soupy mashed potatoes and a pile of boiled beef. The evening meal was the same, except that the potatoes weren't mashed and there was no soup. That beef turned out to be almost the only meat I ate in Ethiopia that was cooked until tender.

An Ethiopian woman brought our food on trays, but with no dessert; the Soviets, forewarned by the meal the day before, had bought bananas and oranges from a fruit stand on the street. Ruslan, gallant host that he was, presented oranges to us peeled part way so that they looked like flowers. The small bananas were also peeled halfway and looked more appetizing than their bruised and blackened skins suggested.

At the end of the noon meal, Sergei pulled out a bottle of vodka and with a quick flourish filled several tumblers halfway full. I noticed the other Americans demurred, claiming they would make their toasts with tea. Because I was new, I felt some obligation to be a comrade. After the first toast, "To the time ahead together," proposed with Sergei's gusto, my glass still wasn't empty. Would he think I was a slacker? Still, drinking straight vodka was a throat-burning experience. Since I had heard one Soviet express disappointment that vodka was not more available in Ethiopia, I declined to let Sergei "fix" my glass. (Ann, in her translation, used that word.) Coyly, I sipped for each of the next boisterous toasts: "To our countries' friendship," "To our work." At the end my glass was empty and I only pretended to drink. Still, returning to our room after lunch, I wobbled.

That first evening in Addis, we Soviets and Americans were curious about the town's night life, so we ventured out together, our nine white faces conspicuous on Addis's streets. We'd heard that the hotel, which towered above the other buildings some five long blocks away, had a restaurant and bar on the top floor. If they couldn't get vodka, the Soviet men were determined to try the local gin.

The hospital gate-keeper let us out through a small door cut in the larger gate. At seven-thirty the streets of Addis were already dark, since near the equator the sun sets early all year long. Along the outside wall of the hospital we passed some ten piles of rags on the packed dirt-and-rock sidewalk. They turned out to be ill and sleeping people. A stifling smell of urine made me want to walk into the street to skirt them, but afraid of seeming callous, I moved instead just beyond their stick-like protruding feet.

After turning the corner, another odor overwhelmed us. Between the curb and the wall was a huge stinking dumpster of food wastes and refuse. The only pleasant smell was that of orange peel, which must have been discarded from fruit bought at several nearby fruit stands. These stands were still open, lit by single electric light bulbs. They displayed oranges, bananas, a few tomatoes, and scrubby potatoes in disorderly piles.

Suddenly a huge unmarked crater some six feet around and deepening to a dark hole loomed in the sidewalk. I saw it just before I might have stepped into it. The price of Addis sidewalks, I decided, is eternal vigilance!

The hotel's elevator wouldn't hold all eight of us. Five of us packed ourselves into its iron-barred cage, quaking while it lifted us tremorously the ten stories to the top. Vladik, Sergei, and Ann suddenly became eager athletes and raced us up the stairs to the top. They joined us, breathless and beaming at their own virtue, while we were negotiating for a table.

The head waiter, hearing that most of us wanted only soda water and Pepsi, demoted us to the plastic-covered tables on the narrow open-air balcony. The anonymity of being out of the way was better for most of us, since we had come as much for the view as for the drinks.

High above the city, with a gentle night breeze blowing, we could lean against a cement railing to peer down at the shadowy structures below. In the hotel's lighted garden restaurant ten stories below us we saw toothpick people moving in couples. Western style dance music floated upward. The scene was one we might have glimpsed from the top of any tall hotel in the U.S.

But this was Ethiopia! It had hit me that afternoon when we saw in a tiny unassuming museum the country's sensation: the three-million-year-old remains of a woman who had died in her twenties. Those bones, nicknamed Lucy, were the oldest human remains ever found. An American paleontologist, Donald Johanson, had found her in 1974 in a parched lake bed two hundred miles northeast of Addis Ababa.

Now, staring out from this hotel balcony I pictured the way she had looked in her display case. Whoever placed her there had supplied her missing bones from plaster reconstructions so that she was a complete tiny skeleton. Impossible! A three-million-year-old woman could not be fit into this pseudo-new world below me.

While the waiter brought my Pepsi, I stood gazing and struck by the lack of any sign of prosperity in this, the capital city of Ethiopia. If Ethiopia's history and archeological treasures could be marketed, dug out like diamonds and somehow sold, I speculated, this country would be rich! But instead, Addis Ababa was a collection of sagging buildings, spotty neon lights, and sparse street lights. The antidote—to look up! The stars shone brightly in a midnight-blue sky, undimmed by urban lights below them. Here on this balcony we were above odors, and the night air was cool with fresh breezes.

Tomorrow we would leave this shabby town. "Our" village, sheltered by these same wide African skies, would surely be cleaner. We had arrived in Ethiopia and . . . it was good.

Overshadowing all we did those first days in Addis Ababa was my curiosity about the camp that would be "home" for the next three months. Prepared for a grim setting, I seized a scrap of hope from the first team's account of the camp's blooming oleander.

It took two vans to transport the nine foreign volunteers and all our gear to Godino. Since no one wanted to sit for sixty kilometers between rucksacks and suitcases, we moved a wood-framed sofa from the FSO office into the seatless space at the back of the van. Luckily, two officials from the Soviet embassy offered to go with us, and so furnished a second van.

Thirteen kilometers from Godino our caravan bumped through Debra Zeit, a city whose main street seemed like a hodgepodge of ramshackle storefronts and corrugated iron shanties. Fred decided it might be useful for the new volunteers to know where Debra Zeit's finest hotel, the Ras Hora, was located. It would soon be our nearest contact with something akin to western civilization.

The hotel parking lot was perched on one of the few tree-shaded hills in Debra Zeit. The restaurant was on a bougainvillea-splashed terrace overlooking a blue volcanic crater lake. Waiters in white coats padded in sandaled feet around the small pool at the center of the courtyard. We filed onto the patio feeling scruffy compared to the hotel's other clientele and found seats at tables in the shade of an arbor bordering the terrace. When we asked about drinks, we learned that soda water, Pepsi, and beer were our choices. I savored the soda water, remembering that thirteen kilometers away I would be drinking only boiled water for three months.

While we sat on the patio, the water-borne echoes of human voices drifted up to our table. I moved to the edge of the terrace and saw four adventurous young men swimming in the lake some hundred feet below. Did their experiment with swimming mean they, like the clientele at the other tables, were better educated and certainly better off than the people we had seen walking Debra Zeit's streets? Would this be one of our last contacts with the "haves" of Ethiopia?

Back in the vans again, our red-ash road crossed a broad sweep of open, scrubby grassland. A high moment! We were finally traveling the last kilometers to Godino. Anticipation was over. What we gazed upon now was "our" territory, the real Ethiopia!

The sky was the same, except there seemed to be a blue beyond the blue of the lid over us. Higher? Deeper. Sunlight glared everywhere, shining through sharp, clear air. The brightness blasted all colors and nearly annihilated them. A single rocky, green-brown mountain loomed in the distance.

The gentle slope of the land between our van and the mountain was dotted with acacia trees which looked like bitten-off sticks. They'd been cut off at the top of the trunk where they branched out. Were the stubs fighting for a second, third— hundredth chance?

Crisscrossing the red-ash road were dried gulleys where wind and rain had eaten away the striated rock. Another season's flash floods had ravaged the land. A blasting sun made these dry gulleys with their scrubby sticks of vegetation look dead.

Long-limbed Ethiopians ambled along the road with dignity. Only a few balanced bundles on their heads, as I had pictured everyone doing. In spite of the blaring sun they wore layers of ragged western-style clothing. For protection? Most of the men wore straw hats woven of sisal. All of the women had scarves tied about their heads. Some boys were bare-headed, but more often they wore straw hats or beaten-up baseball caps perched rakishly on their heads. Girls were mostly bare-headed above their loose-hanging faded frocks. Some folk had donkeys to carry their loads. Most walked in twos and threes, scattering to the side of the road to watch as our vehicle passed. Some waved, others seemed to hope for a ride until they saw that our van was already heavily loaded.

One ancient tree, stark in this barren landscape, stood alone beside the road. It was a huge spreading oak, its leaves clumped on broad branches off a gnarled trunk. A tree of life? How had it survived? Who had protected it in a landscape where the other sparse trees, mostly acacias, looked as if they had been axed off?

A while later, we came upon a huge grader spreading red gravel from a nearby volcanic ash site. How did Ethiopia afford such huge machinery, I wondered, and were its drivers willing to work on a Sunday? Later I learned that the skill to operate such machinery makes a man unique in this country, and work is so scarce that anytime he can get it, he'll probably be willing to work. As the van bumped and swayed over the piles of gravel the grader made, I hoped that our future trips would be less rough and dusty, thanks to this Sunday laborer.

At last the village of Godino could be seen ahead. Instead of continuing, however, the van turned off onto two dusty ruts which shortly ran through the sparse water of a small stream. Once we had forded the stream the van plunged up the bank and reached a rugged spot where it could lurch along the patchy stone paving of an old Italian-built road. I spied two large holes amongst the scrubby vegetation, which later I learned were porcupine holes.

And our camp? It was a shaded oasis! It lay on a rise of ground split by a gulley and a good-sized stream. A Russian settler in the early 1900s had planted a cluster of trees—eucalyptus, jacaranda, acacia—around several small buildings that comprised his home. The trees had been spared, left to grow tall and protective. Our camp would glean the benefit of their shade.

We arrived at the camp's corrugated-iron gate, which was opened by a one-eyed guard, Aklilu, who was dressed in a tee-shirt and cut-off pants. Our two vans drove just inside the gate and stopped. A young very black Ethiopian man approached our van. It was the team captain, Belay. We had arrived!

The camp was a clutter of ten tents plus two outbuildings—a kitchen house and the wash house/latrine. Dingy corrugated iron buildings are found everywhere in Ethiopia, but our kitchen and latrine were of iron new enough to be shiny.

The camp was arranged in two rows. One held seven tents. Facing the bright-colored new tents were the wash-house, a *tukel* or mud hut, and three old canvas storage tents. In the fifty-foot space between the two rows, a clothesline hung low. High and crowning the whole area, a line sported the flags of our three countries: Ethiopia, the Soviet Union, and the U.S.A.

Fencing most of the camp were the blooming bushes we'd heard about. Fancy! Instead of thorny acacia, our camp sported colorful oleander and bougainvillae for fencing; oleander leaves were poisonous to cows, who were smart enough to leave them alone. Ploughshares had provided several Hilary-type tents large enough to hold two iron cots with thick foam rubber mattresses. Jack and I could push our two beds together for low-voiced nighttime speculation and kibitzing.

Showers? Latrines? I wanted to see everything, so Pam joined me in exploring. She seemed proud of the shower arrangement at one end of the wash house. For a shower, you filled a large plastic bucket with a plastic tube at its base and hoisted it just above your head using a pulley system. Then, whenever you pulled down the nozzle at its base, gravity made cold water flow from it. If you wanted warm water, a bag made of thick plastic could be filled three or four hours ahead of time and placed out in the sun. Ethiopia's sun was powerful enough to rapidly heat the water to bathwater temperature. Cold water worked well for everything but hair-washing. On a given afternoon, three of us at a time would wash our hair, making do with one bag of warm water.

The latrines were two chambers at the far end of the corrugated iron wash house. Each chamber sported a square hole set in its cement floor, which was surrounded on three sides by a two-inch high cement platform for one's feet. Rolls of coarse, pink toilet paper, which the camp had wrangled from Balcha Hospital hung from a string in each of the chambers. Pam suggested that, because t.p. was in such short supply, the westerners practice using water to wash, as Ethiopians did. (During the three months, certain supplies chronically came up short. We were always "nearly out" of toilet paper.)

Large cement sinks in the open center of the wash house served as tubs for washing ourselves and our clothes. Their water flowed from another plastic bucket with a spray nozzle. Just beside the wash house a huge iron drum served as our water storage tank.

While we stood near the wash house, a fifteen-year-old boy arrived driving a donkey with two plastic water cannisters on either side of its back. Pam used gestures to introduce him as Wandosun. This young man, a kind of "man-about-camp," did all kinds of chores for us. His main task was to fill the water depot twice a day by driving the donkey a quarter of a mile to the stream. The water from the stream was clean enough to wash with, but he also brought drinking water enough to fill a large plastic storage depot in the kitchen after the cooks had boiled it. When asked to, Wandosun also dashed water onto the latrine floors to clean them. He also bought food from the village, things like bananas, eggs, and live chickens when they were available.

That first night in camp, we wanted to begin to explore the village. Fred suggested we follow a hardened earth trail that led to our water source. As the group ambled beside a farmer's field I noticed how tough and sun-baked were its earth-clods. Where irrigation water had run between the rows, the earth had cracked and formed a pattern of saucer-sized black rectangles. No wonder it was hard to dig this earth! When ploughed it might be productive, but now the fields appeared to be cloaked in a tough leathery hide.

As we walked, our group collected a coterie of dusty-legged children, curious and smiling. Tentatively, they tried phrases. "Vat ees yoh name?" Then they tried to say our names. "Judeee . . . Anneee . . . Rooslan." Carefully, they repeated the easier ones. The sounds were strange to them. We tried some of their names: "Emebet . . . Gera . . . Kasu," names equally odd to us. Slowly we made our way, jumping onto the low rocks of the stream bed. A few curious village men joined us.

The brass-gold light of the evening hour gave the gulley where the piped stream-head flowed a magic aura. From that pipe water came in a steady stream for all the Godino villagers. A gathering of some ten children and an equal number of adults hung about this particular evening, somehow acknowledging with their presence their need for this flowing, steady, sparkling stream. Fred told us in English as we stood watching the water that Gowa, the other village where we worked, had no pipe. As a result, there were steady squabbles about how close to the head of their stream, which bubbled from the ground, families should wash their clothes. Our teammate Senbet told us that Mageera, a village some three kilometers away from this stream, had no water at all. When the Mageera folk needed water they had to carry it three kilometers either from Godino or Gowa. I never returned to that pipe during our stay in camp, but I knew where Wandosun and his donkey had to go to bring our water. This water had been basic to these villagers' existence their entire lives. It would be basic to mine for the next three months. I felt reverent.

That first night dusk fell about 6:30 P.M., just as it was to fall every night of the three months we lived there. Because the camp was located eight degrees off the equator, nights and days were of almost equal length. Sunsets flashed color across the earth and sky, but they were never long and lingering. At the first bruise of night, reflected light from the pink clouds lit the shiny corrugated iron buildings of our camp and made the canvas of our tents glow. When there were no clouds a brief pink-gold brassy light lit the world. Then the dark inked it out.

Of all the experiences of Ethiopia, the nights were the most captivating to me. Neither the village nor our camp sported electricity to blur the night sky. Clear stars formed myriad constellations. At around eight we could usually find a satellite star moving across the top of the vast sky's bowl. Toward morning, we could find the Southern Cross, a bright kite in the equatorial sky.

That first night, lying awake in our tent, I heard the sounds of the African night as I would seldom hear them again. I had expected that the silence would be vast beneath the wide star-studded bowl of the sky. I was wrong. What I heard was better than silence. A breeze lowed in the trees above our tent. The wind was accompanied by a warm symphony of sound: the whirring hum of insects, a chorus of crickets punctuated by an individual chirper beeping in what I guessed was B-flat.

Dogs barked in the village across the stream. At some moments only one lone hound signalled his unease with a yip. At other times the howl of a hyena roused every mutt in the village and sparked a cacophony. Occasionally a donkey's bray joined the ruckus.

I lay that night in the darkness and thought about what I had seen of these villagers. I had sensed a certain fresh quality in their lives. They seemed attractive, unsophisticated, and vulnerable. Their way of life appeared at the same time happy-go-lucky and solid. It would never be possible for me to live as they did, but to be brushed by their simplicity for just these three months would be a gift.

Just how primitive, I wondered, was rural Ethiopia? Did the supernatural haunt the rural folk here? The images of this area had given me a sense of the preternatural, rather than the supernatural: myriad natural phenomena, close, raw, relentless. In Ethiopia nature had already begun to implode me.

Toward morning a single rooster's crow, the harbinger of dawn, sounded from our neighbor's house across the path and just over the fence, and I awoke. Our camp was perched on a rise across the stream from the main village, but the village head, his wife, their four small sons, and domestic animals were our near neighbors. Their rooster had beat the birds out, but the three-toned mourning cry of a dove and the twitter of weavers soon announced that other birds were also alive and skittering.

In the early morning semi-darkness I heard men's voices calling to each other. They made no effort to hush their tones. Then someone sang. Was it a camp guard supporting a fellow guard's attempt to stay awake? Since there was no electricity in camp and reading by candle or flashlight was difficult, I could tell I would be retiring early. Since I didn't actually need to sleep ten hours, wakefulness was going to be rich!

3.
Why Work When
You Can Celebrate?

THAT first morning in camp I took a full breath of clean village air, and felt ready to go to work. The actual work had been described to us only in vague terms until we reached camp. Now it was becoming more clear. We were to join FSO in teaching the villagers methods of enriching their soil. In addition we had seeds to give them, which would make their diet more varied.

Why was this important? Because drought always threatened Ethiopia with famine, and the limited crops the farmers grew presently did not give their diet adequate vitamins and minerals. The farmers in Godino had been given land in small garden plots, but few of them knew how to make their land truly productive. Machinery was not only unavailable to work their plots, but impractical for smaller gardens. The organic methods FSO was introducing required back-breaking work, but it was work the farmers could do themselves with the hope of improving their yields.

Our aim was to show the farmers how to better use the limited space around their houses to dig twenty-four inches deep into the ground to loosen the soil so it would grow better vegetables. Even in Amharic, the beds we encouraged them to prepare were called "double digs," because usually village farmers dug their beds only twelve inches deep.

Besides double digs, we planned to demonstrate how to make and use compost. We were told most Ethiopian soil would also need sand added to enrich it. We needed to make ourselves as knowledgeable about these organic methods as we could. Once a farmer had done the initial heavy digging, the theory was that he would have productive beds in which to plant and re-plant vegetables. We had carrot, beet, and head-cabbage seeds (all new to these farmers) to give them as a reward for doing the initial heavy work of preparing their double-dig beds.

But the first day in camp was January 7, which was also the most important day of the Coptic Christian year: Christmas. Belay, the Ethiopian captain of our team, explained that first morning that the holiday would postpone the start of our work. Belay had black, black skin and a wonderfully rounded head of hair. Since the whites of his eyes matched his white teeth, his appearance made me think of an eager, grinning small boy, the kind who appears in advertisements for toothpaste. There was nothing "small boy" about Belay, however, except his enthusiasm. That first morning he grinned and asked, "Is anyone curious to see a Christmas celebration?" He himself was not an orthodox Christian, he was an evangelical Christian, but he would accompany whoever was willing to walk the three kilometers to a tiny village called Mageera and back.

The three younger Soviets, Sergei, Vladislov, and Olga, along with Ann, Jack, and I, decided to brave the long, hot walk. ("Mad dogs and Englishmen go out in the midday sun.") Another teammate, Senbet, offered to be a second guide. At ten o'clock, under a cloud cover that seemed to threaten rain, we struck out across the dry plain. Instantly, I saw I'd been naive to come bare-headed. I had neither hat nor umbrella to shelter me from the sun, which appeared to be about to beat out the clouds.

Emerging from behind a small hill, off in the distance across a dusty, sparse-grassed plain we saw a tiny church huddled on the crown of a hill. We had been out about twenty minutes when the sun burst from the clouds, and beat on our bare heads as mercilessly as it beat at the hard, cracked and eroded earth beneath us.

But Belay was unflagging. He announced that a rocky dry river gorge was "all" that lay between us and the Mageera church's hill. "All" looked like a lot to me, but it was Christmas. I trudged toward that hill feeling like a weary wise man.

Belay, Jack, and I began to chat. Senbet, Olga, Sergei, and Vladik (our nickname for Vladislov) distracted themselves with Ann, since she spoke both Russian and English. Clearly, twenty-one-year-old Vladik was fascinated by this lovely twenty-five-year-old North American volunteer to whom he could speak and be understood. I suspected Senbet of a similar interest.

Belay led us along the top edge of the dry river gorge, and I began to look ahead for trees where we could pause for shade. I saw only one spreading tree that had missed being chopped off at the top. It must have had no thorns so that its branches were of no use for fencing. We made a bee line for its shady oasis.

Belay waited for us standing high on a rock that was still out in the sun. He wore no hat. Playfully, I called him brave, and he smiled. "My black skin is better than yours—like asbestos, heat- and sun-resistant," he bragged.

When we were walking once again, I asked Belay about his childhood. "My father was rich—he owned a hundred cows," he began. Belay was one of the last of his father's sons, but when he was only six his father died. He was left alone with his mother, who could not fend off the raids of his many older brothers born to the father's other wives. Upon hearing of the death of their father, a host of these brothers came home and took off all the cattle, and suddenly Belay and his mother were poor. Missionaries helped Belay's mother, and with that help he was able to continue in school. But no one had protected Belay and his mother from the aching struggle of poverty.

Belay, his father's youngest son and clearly special to him, started school at an early age. "I may have been too young. I did not do well that first year." At the end of the year the school director informed little Belay that he would have to repeat the first grade. Failure was a new experience for the small boy, and he cried and carried on. How could he be separated from his first-grade friends who would be in second grade the following year? So when school began after the brief summer vacation, Belay joined his classmates in the second grade as if he belonged there. The school's director was summoned to pluck the child out and put him back into first grade. Belay resisted, and the director sent him home, whereupon an angry father returned to the school with his son.

"My father, who was an illiterate landlord," Belay told us, "came and scolded the director and also blamed all the teachers, saying that his son so clever and never likes lazy children." The father's rage was explosive enough to make the teachers reconsider. Young Belay was given an exam to see if he could read. Fortunately, he was asked to read aloud a story he already knew. Though he didn't know how to read, he pretended he did, recited the story to the examining assembly, and was admitted to the second grade.

But soon after Belay was promoted his father died. Five years later, his mother also died. "I wept and wept and wept for Mom! I thought I knew better than anyone else that my tears would do her good. *Haaae!* I wept and drained my tears completely for I have never had tears to weep since then."

Belay continued in school. In 1982 he got his degree in agriculture. He followed that, as many Ethiopians do, by traveling to the Soviet Union to study for a higher degree in economics.

Jobs followed. At first he worked with the Ethiopian Ministry of Agriculture as a planner and then as a general agricultural instructor. He had also been a project manager for World Vision International, a large and well-funded relief organization that has carried out agricultural projects in many areas of Ethiopia. But he left World Vision, taking a cut in pay, because he was idealistically challenged to work with Family Service Organization. Belay was attracted to FSO for several reasons. It was small and solely Ethiopian. In addition, it made a difference to him that the Ethiopians working in it were dedicated Christians, determined to initiate and carry out agricultural demonstration projects.

Belay turned, looked me straight in the eye, and asked if in this sun I was ready for a history lesson. I attempted enthusiasm. Any distraction was welcome. He explained that sustainable agriculture was important because, when the Derg, the army officers who deposed Haile Selassie, had set about implementing their Marxist policies, one of their first decrees was a rural land reform. Villagers received small plots of land and were required to live in villages rather than dispersed on the larger tracts they cultivated. City families could keep one dwelling. Banks, insurance companies, and most foreign investments were nationalized.

But as early as the 1960s, the Eritreans in the north had begun to agitate for independence, and the government that had evolved from the Derg's takeover, like Haile Selassie's government before it, had been distracted from its reforms in order to meet rebel pressures.

The Derg also suffered from internal problems, and after a shoot-out in 1977, a young man who called himself Comrade Mengistu Haile Mariam emerged as the Derg's new chairman. However, waging war in the north and maintaining power in the rest of Ethiopia kept Mengistu from making further reforms. The ministry of agriculture was given little money and had minimal power to help villagers learn better farming methods.

Villagers saw the Mengistu government as a bureacracy that sent men into the villages every few months to kidnap young males for the war front. The village powers were ordered to seize young men for the army or go to prison themselves. Belay's voice nearly bleated as he described how able-bodied males between fifteen and twenty were taken off without warning or a chance to say goodbye. They received military training for six months, then went to the front. A soldier got no respite from the battle lines until he was maimed or killed.

At last we arrived at the base of the hill with the church at its top and joined a gathering of villagers trudging up the slope. They wore holiday finery: cardigans over dresses made of shiny fabrics in bright new colors. Even in the heat, many men wore sweaters or worn sports jackets. Many of the women wore a white shawl to cover their heads, but on this occasion there were no white cotton shawls draped over the men's shoulders as I had seen in Addis. Shawls were reserved for the priests, none of whom had yet appeared when we arrived at the top of the hill for a service scheduled to have started an hour before. Most of the men wore hats woven of sisal with bands of bright-colored yarn. A few of the poorer men and boys wore their old dusty, ragged hats. But on this holiday most of the disreputable hats had been left at home. Bright hats and colors reigned.

At the top of the hill we joined other villagers already seated and waiting in the shade of the verandah that ran around the entire circular church. Belay mysteriously disappeared, and Senbet took his place as our chief interpreter and guide. He reminded us that just over half of all Ethiopians are Coptic Christians and that about 10 percent of the country is Islamic.

When we asked about where the Coptic Church had come from, he told us the story he'd heard: scattered references to Ethiopia in the Old Testament have led to a legend that the Queen of Sheba visited King Solomon and he seduced her. When she later gave birth to a son, Menelik I, the Solomonic Dynasty began its rule in Ethiopia and lasted until Haile Selassie's fall in 1974.

Legend traces the first Ethiopian Coptic Christians to the fourth-century conversion of Ethiopia's inhabitants from Judaism and paganism to Christianity. The new religion spread when "Nine Syrian Saints" arrived at the end of the fifth century and founded churches and monasteries.

This village church was small and unassuming, Senbet told us, compared to the rock-hewn churches built in the twelfth century by a Christian King named Lalibela. I had seen pictures of these churches carved into deep pits in the earth. There, on the top of the hill observing the tiny church, I thought not only of those huge rock-hewn churches, but also of Christian cathedrals. In the twelfth century Ethiopian Coptic Orthodox Christians had spent enormous energy hewing their cathedrals out of rock downward from the ground's surface at the same time that European Christians were erecting their cathedrals to spire upward. In Addis I had asked if we could see these churches carved out of rock, and had been disappointed to learn I couldn't. Lalibela was in the northern province of Wollo, a war zone.

The mumblings of the crowd indicated the priests would arrive at some vague time to begin the ceremony. Most people were standing. All of us white-skinned foreigners were beginning to wish we could be less conspicuous. Besides, I was tired and longed to sit somewhere instead of standing. I looked for and found a small tree to sit under just off the brow of the hill beside a shack-like building of corrugated iron. Looking uphill as I sat, my eyes fell on the circular Coptic cross at the top of the church. It was the one decorative effort on that plain, hexagonal, wooden building.

While I gazed at the church, I was aware of the eyes of children standing at a not overly discreet distance to stare at me: a white-skinned faranji, a woman who wore pants. Was I offending by wearing pants at a Christmas celebration? No one showed signs of disapproval. An occasional adult, aware that the children's relentless stares might be considered rude, came to scatter them. After those scoldings for a time the older children and young adults stole only furtive glances, but they did not move off. Some of the young entrepreneurs sold their bits of gum and candy to the other children more assiduously.

The wait—the service finally started at noon—gave me time to snap pictures from my sitting position. Several photos I took show a flock of villagers standing stiffly, looking straight at the camera. They seemed eager to be recorded.

At last we heard that the priests had arrived and gone into the church. They would soon come out for a procession in which the faithful would follow them as they paraded about the hill singing and dancing.

We were told that the inside of the church was considered too sacred for ordinary folk to enter, and then we received a message. The holy men wished to conduct the faranjis on a tour of the inner sanctuary. We were disinclined to separate ourselves from the rest of the villagers by accepting a special privilege, but with some hesitation we moved toward the church. Senbet came along reluctantly to provide translation.

After removing our shoes, we were ushered inside and around the dark, empty circular corridor past six inner altars. The central altar was hexagonal in shape and each of its six sides was draped in a plain brown curtain hanging from above and fastened with safety pins. A lone candle cast an eerie light on each of the religious pictures hanging on the draped panels—"The Last Supper," "Christ in the Garden of Gethsemene"—all scenes from the life of Christ and his mother.

Ethiopians particularly venerate Mary, we heard, and these pictures illustrated that emphasis. They understand her to be not only the mother of Jesus, but also the mother of God. She is the merciful being, the bestower of all goodness, to whom supplications are offered. They ask Mary to help them prosper, have children, and be healed. Slowly, we shuffled around the circle over the straw-strewn dirt floor. At the close of our tour a priest explained why we'd been allowed to see the inner sanctuary. The church elders wanted us to see that the church had only a dirt floor. They were hoping for our help to pave it!

When we were ushered out of the church we stooped to put our shoes back on. Four of the priests stayed inside to don bright-colored brocaded robes for the procession. I hung about with my camera at the door of the church. While I was focusing on one white-turbaned priest, I thought I saw him frown. Thinking he did not want his picture taken, I diverted the camera. But the priest nabbed Senbet—indeed he did want his picture taken, Senbet reported. The frown indicated his hope that he would get a copy of it!

While we waited with the crowd milling about just outside the church, an old gap-toothed priest wearing a raincoat and a gauze turban took Senbet by the arm and pulled him to us to translate. "Thank you for coming," he said. "We speak a different language, and our skin color is different, but we are all sons of Adam."

I'd been called a son of Adam. If my gender meant nothing to this priest, it meant nothing to me. Until he spoke to me I had felt like a stranger. But this old man made me feel somehow initiated.

The procession seemed so traditional that it must have been in place since Coptic Christianity came to Ethiopia in the fourth century. A small boy emerged from the church carrying a Coptic cross. Another boy came out carrying a picture of Christ removed temporarily from one of the altars inside. Then two bearded priests emerged, each supporting a heavy brocaded rectangular frame over his head and wearing a long embroidered robe. They were flanked by two colorfully robed, turbaned men holding silver-embroidered umbrellas; these were both decorative and useful in shielding the heavily dressed priests from the sun. Majestically, to the beat of drums, the procession moved down the hill.

Suddenly we heard loud gun shots, and the four priests stopped. Then there took place in front of the brocaded priests a ceremony in which a young priest slit the throats of two goats. I watched in awe, aware of how ancient this rite of sacrifice is in religious celebration. One goat struggled wildly, his red-rimmed eye open and fiery, while his blood poured out onto the ground. Then, solemnly, the stately robed men passed on around the scene, and the dead goats were left lying in the dust to be cut up and apportioned out later.

When the procession reached a flat space beneath a tree, partway down the hill, it stopped. The four brocaded priests stood in a straight line facing the crowd. A devotee spread out a long narrow rug for them to stand on. Some ten other turbaned priests with long sticks began to shake their brass rattles and move in a circle, dancing and chanting to a drum beat. Their slow rhythms and slurred words indicated they were probably well fortified with the local brew, *tala*.

After some minutes the monotonous swaying and chanting ended, and the company moved back up the hill. The brocaded priests left, and a horde of men moved to the rug, where they knelt and kissed the sacred spot where the holy ones had stood. Since the Soviets seemed restless, sun-weary, and eager to leave, this appeared to be a time to gracefully slip away.

Farther down the hill we passed some young men gathered under another large tree. Brandishing sturdy sticks, they danced more vigorously than the priests had. Their singing voices were livelier and louder. Were they somehow in competition with the other ceremony? Still farther down, a third group of very young boys was shaking sticks and jumping about wildly. They appeared to be mimicking the second group as if to say, "If you won't let us join you big guys, we can imitate you."

Walking home across the hot plain, we felt we had witnessed a color and celebration rare in village life, but of course we had no previous experience with which to compare it.

Belay led us home by way of Gowa, the other village near our camp. He wanted to show us how villages had been laid out by the government in the late 1970's when it passed its "villagization" decree. In that reform the government gave each villager a thousand-square-meter plot of land on which to build his house, and required that all persons live in a village rather than on separate, larger plots. Though it had limited water, Gowa was an energetic village, Belay claimed. Many of its farmers had done "double digs" and had begun to grow vegetables on the land about their houses.

The path wound down into the gorge we had skirted earlier. Since rocks and a steep slope made our way slippery, Sergei offered me his arm. I didn't think I needed his help, but I wanted to respond to his gallantry, and so I took him up on it. Nearing the bottom, I slipped and nearly fell, and Sergei caught me. "Sergei saved me," I told the others playfully. He understood enough English to be delighted.

Later, when we finally reached the top of the gorge, Sergei stopped, breathless, and asked Olga to translate. "We are young, but we are tired, too," he reported, as if it were important that I know he, too, was tired. Weeks later, when I appeared to have more endurance for work in the fields than Sergei, I wondered if he still thought of me as so much older and weaker than he was.

That evening we celebrated. Viva to our first full day in camp! The Soviets also felt festive, because it was the Russian Orthodox Christmas. Olga told me her family in Moscow would be celebrating their first Christmas in many years. Here, the cooks were off for Christmas. The Soviets opened cans of the specialties they had brought from the USSR. There were sardines, and someone had brought a small can of caviar. Olga opened it in the kitchen and arranged small black piles on hunks of coarse Ethiopian bread the cook had baked and left us. Sergei even brought out a string of salami.

It was dark by the time we gathered at our three eating tables, arranged end to end outside the kitchen under a canvas awning. We ate with a single light bulb hanging above our tables, powered by a noisy, gasoline-run Soviet generator. The generator's clatter was so loud we could scarcely hear each other as we spoke our toasts: "To friendship," "To the return of Christmas celebrations to Moscow," "To the start of our work together." That was the first and only night we had champagne. Some made their toasts with vodka, some with champagne, and our Ethiopian teammates quietly stuck with tea.

Already we were aware of, and perhaps a bit subdued by, Ethiopian shortages of gasoline, sugar, meat. Nonetheless, that first night we squandered our luxuries and put a jolly face on our toasts. Later, if we had to we would face up to shortages.

When the food was gone, we lingered around the table. There was no light anywhere else in camp, and it was only seven-thirty, We couldn't go to bed! That night became the first occasion for a dinner time ritual. We chose one person and, complete with translation, we heard his or her life story. That first night Fred Bauman gave us a preview by telling about himself, since he and Pam would soon be leaving.

I was asked to sing and teach the group what later became a regular camp song: "Dona Nobis Pacem." Its words are simple for a group with mixed languages since the three Latin words of its title are its only lyrics. Everyone liked the sentiment of the words, "Give Us Peace," but our rusty singing voices, coaxed from our throats after long disuse, sounded like a chorus of frogs. Practice, that's what we needed! Practice singing, practice digging, practice making do.

4.
Ah, Compost!

THE Ploughshares application had specifically stated, "No skills needed." I had told everyone, "I'm going to Africa to dig ditches." When we actually arrived and found we were to use and demonstrate bio-intensive organic agriculture, I was floored. "Training will come in the field; the trick is to be creative and flexible," they had said. Dealing with life in the United States had made me think I was resourceful and creative. But living abroad had already taught me how foreign countries can displace all my ordinary virtues and make a stubborn, nagging crone out of a usually good-natured me. I just hoped I could adjust!

Belay, who had a good deal of agricultural savvy, was to train us. Pam, who was clearly an "organic buff" was to help. Pam did most of the formal class training. She set up a portable blackboard under the shading canvas at the head of the two eating tables and drew the layers of a compost pile for us. Then she described what to put in those layers and why we should make compost. What I recall of that session was Pam's amazingly well-manicured fingers when she gestured: "Run your fingers through your compost when it's finished. Love it," she told us. "To make compost is as close as you'll ever come to working a miracle."

Ah, Compost!

She won us over. The distractions—swatting at fly-clusters on the table, the heat, the people steadily passing our outdoor classroom—couldn't overpower her enthusiasm. I took notes, which I never glanced at again, but I did embrace the organic idea. Our recruiters were right: the real learning would happen in the doing.

The first work morning, Belay led us to two long grassy spaces in the camp's 1,000-meter large demonstration garden. One thousand meters square had been chosen as our demonstration size since the plots villagers had been given by the government were that size. "We'll make these into double digs," he announced as he stood at the head of two long plots. This meant loosening the top twelve inches with a garden fork, ridding the ground of its network of grass roots, digging the dirt out a good foot further down, adding manure and sand, and turning it all back into a raised bed ready for planting. In preparing these beds we would learn the technique and experience the energy a double dig demanded. The training worked. I developed a healthy respect for the work required from any village farmer willing to do the heavy digging necessary to make his earth more productive for growing vegetables.

Hot sun is a given in Ethiopia. Those first mornings we straggled out to the field at about eight-thirty, when it was still cool. Sergei was usually the last. Ruslan was often late; he held an informal clinic by the wash house almost every morning, once the villagers learned there was a doctor in camp. An odd clinic it was, requiring two translators—one to translate from English into Russian, and an Ethiopian teammate to translate complaints and suggestions between English and Amharic for the patient. But when Ruslan examined and dressed wounds, his caring communicated without language.

"You have to have manure," Pam had said. If fresh manure were needed to stimulate the decomposition process in our compost heap, we had to have it. The second day we drove in the huge gas-guzzling truck donated by the Soviet

43

Union over to the International Livestock Center for Africa (ILCA). The trip had two aims: to meet ILCA's staff and to get permission to shovel away some of the research center's ample store of cow dung.

Compost making had a colorful initiation. The morning we started we arrived to dig the pit near where Arba, an older Ethiopian man, and two young boys were sifting the dirt from another nearly decomposed compost pile. Arba was shoveling the compost into a wire net sifter crudely made from four sticks tied together in a rectangle. He was delighted to stop work, shake hands, and introduce himself. Jack pointed questioningly to a pin in the lapel of Arba's dirt-matted sport jacket that bore the insignia of the Soviet Peace Fund. Suddenly, the old gentleman came alive. Someone on the previous team must have given the pin to him.

Notice of that pin was what Arba seemed to be waiting for. He held one finger in the air to indicate he considered the pin a first prize, won from the first team's Soviets. Then he began to dance. With leaps, contortions, and rapid shaking of his shoulders, Arba made it clear that he might be sixty-five years old, but the spirit had not forsaken his prize-winning dance!

Arba's contortions stimulated the two young boys to match him. One of the boys grabbed the Ethiopian-style fork I was using, which was shaped like a pick-axe with three tines to use for breaking the soil. Swinging the fork, he began to chop away vigorously at the soil where we needed a pit for the compost. The ground was hard! His energy flagged. The second boy took his turn. Shortly, their enthusiasm waned and we all took up our respective tasks. But our work that morning had started with an enthusiastic initiation.

Making compost heaps turned out to be one of my favorite pastimes. To take unused vegetation and manure and put it into a pile that will later become so very productive is satisfying. Pam had told us to think about how life-giving the compost was to the soil. That morning I looked at the cow-dung piled at our site. If later that smelly stuff

44

could stimulate the straw, green leaves, kitchen waste, and ash we were layering into the pile to become loose black dirt it might indeed be one of nature's major miracles. Ah yes, I might even run my fingers through that loose loam and love it!

The problem with making compost in Ethiopia with its hot sun and sparse water is to keep it moist enough to feed the process of decay. After the heap is made, its major requirement is moisture, and our watering pond was a long way from the heaps. We carried water to the compost in watering cans, but we also urged men to feel free to go to the pile and urinate on it. Together with the cow dung, urine would help keep it moist and aid the pile's bacterial activity.

For that first compost pile, the green matter layer was hardest to find. Given our pile's large size, the kitchen waste we'd collected—which with Ethiopia's diet is neither abundant nor varied—was meager. January was the heart of the dry season, so each time we needed a layer of green matter, several of us would go down to the dry creek bed near the site and tear green leaves off the trees.

Part of the pleasure of the work those early weeks was learning about our fellow workers. When Olga and I found ourselves foraging for green material together one morning, we continued a chat we'd begun the day before while sitting on the cot in her tent, where we'd been looking at pictures of our families. Now there was time for detail. Yes, Olga was an economist for a Moscow tourist agency, but she seemed to have more interest in things like knitting and cooking than she did in her job. Her husband, who she said was a "new-style" man in Moscow, had worked for Aeroflot and had taken many flights outside the Soviet Union. When Olga applied and was selected to come to Ethiopia with the Soviet Peace Fund, her husband encouraged her. He wanted his wife to have the same travel advantages he had enjoyed. "He said," she claimed proudly, "it was my turn to go. He promise to look to Sasha (their seven-year-old son). I was not to worry. Everything be fine."

I asked Olga about the long queues and shortages in the Soviet Union. "I am optimist. Last long, they do not," she said. "Some item will be short for ten days, then we have again. My mother-in-law, she get very upset when things are not found. I am more easy. I cannot bother myself to stand in line for a different cheese, when there is one cheese at home. Only I wait for the shortage to end." I wondered if the Soviet shortages would make our Ethiopian shortages easier for her.

I looked at Olga to signal my appreciation for her attitude and noticed that even at work she was wearing heavy eyeliner. The incongruity of wearing make-up in a physical work situation made me question my ideas about the Soviet Union. Never having been there, I had taken my ideas about the material shortages of everyday life from the media, and imagined life in the USSR to be dramatically difficult. Now, speaking with someone who knew the whole of everyday life in the Soviet Union, I recognized that the difficulties in that country were the same as difficulties anywhere. They were only as disarming as one took them to be.

While gleaning green leaves I thought about the huge piles of grass clippings in our compost pile back home. An abundant supply of grass made our compost different. Grass clippings made the pile steamy hot after we mowed our lawn, but it became so airless that the thick black mouldering mat had to be broken up regularly.

Earthworms were also abundant in our compost at home. Turning the pile over always uncovered several tangles of worms—an inedible squirming mass of red spaghetti. In Ethiopia, we never once saw an earthworm. We were told that was why fresh dung was so essential. Manure helped produce the bacteria which in turn would break down the pile's materials into dirt.

One day while we were adding the contents of an older compost pile to our double-dig bed, I noticed Belay and Pam engaged in a prolonged, mildly animated argument which appeared to be about compost. Overhearing scraps of it, I learned that Pam was expressing her disappointment that

Belay had used the compost in the double-dig beds before it had fully decomposed. Belay claimed it was better to use compost that was not quite ready than no compost at all, claiming that it continued to decompose while it was in the bed. Later that night I heard Pam pressing the same point to Belay in the next tent. When, the following morning, Belay and I were breaking up clods of dry chicken manure for compost, I told him I had overheard the conversation and sympathized with him. "It's a good thing that living in Ethiopia, as you do, you're not a perfectionist," I said. "If you were, you'd be constantly frustrated."

Belay looked as though he didn't know the meaning of "frustrated." "Pam takes her position," I continued, "because in the U.S. we sometimes have the luxury of trying to do things perfectly, but the perfect may be the enemy of the good." Those were the words that came out of my mouth, but I wasn't sure what I meant by them. Living more basically in this Ethiopian village, I knew there were basic differences in this simpler way of life, but I couldn't yet articulate what they were. Often my logic emerges when I have to explain what I mean about something, so I tried to put into words what I meant by "the luxury of perfection" we had in the U.S.

"The computer has burst onto the U.S. scene in the last ten years," I began. "With computers we can calculate, study, and do more things more thoroughly than we've ever been able to before. Technology has invaded our medicine, our agriculture, our research—everything. A great many more perfect answers are possible to us in the U.S. today. And because we can aim for and achieve results closer to perfection, often we're not satisfied with anything less than 'the perfect.' Only occasionally do we think how the perfect may be the enemy of the good. In Ethiopia, for instance, if you wait for perfectly decomposed compost, you may put off using partially ready compost, and your crops may never get the benefit of 'good' compost."

I'm not sure I made my point clearly enough for Belay,

but his answer was gracious. "Ah, yes, compost." Without repeating how he felt about using compost, he said, "Pam's such a good Christian that she needs to talk out any disagreement until it's resolved."

I found that to fork the hard earth into tenderness for double digging required a new motion. If I wanted to make the garden fork penetrate deeply, I had to jump on it. However, after a few jumps in that awkward dance it was clear to our teammates that the women might be more effective loosening grass roots. Henceforth, our male teammates took over the garden forks for the major digging and left Anne and Olga and me to do the lighter jobs.

The job I liked was softening the earth by watering the beds and letting the water soak in. The first team had dug a pond where the project collected water the three days a week that water ran down the irrigation troughs into our demonstration field. It was no ordinary pond. On a small island in its center grew a small acacia tree: the first team had planted flower seeds at the tree's base so that the tiny island was a steady spot of color in the middle of our garden. From that reservoir we could either dip water out to pour from galvinized steel watering cans, or fill a large steel drum perched on the pond's edge. A plastic hose running from the drum could be pulled to varying parts of the demonstration garden. That hose was the closest we came to any mechanical device. Most of the time we found it easier to simply dip watering cans into the pond and lug them to the fields.

One tractor owned by the government was available to the members of the local farmers' association to use in turns. But our Ethiopian teammates purposely plowed our *teff* (the local grain) field by hitching two oxen to a wooden yoke. The aim was to use only those methods available to the local farmers, who had such infrequent access to mechanical aids.

Another process we performed was the sifting of compost to make it ready for planting. We planted demonstration fruit and vegetable seedlings in pure compost. For sifting we used a crude wire screen strung across sticks which two boys held and shook. To help farmers still more, we had sturdy hand tools available to lend to those who agreed to do double digs. The design of our U.S.-made tools seemed better to some of the farmers, but others preferred to use the tools they were used to.

One late morning we were in the field working slowly while we waited for the noon break to come. I heard the van arrive in camp, and soon afterward on the center stone path of our demonstration garden there appeared a stranger's face. It was pale.

"Noel! Noel's come back," Pam cried. Noel had been with the first team for the month of October. He had left hoping to come back after raising the money to support himself while on the project. He was back now to stay and make a fourth on the U.S. team. (Pam and Fred would soon return to the U.S.) Noel knew Russian well, which made him a still more valuable member of our team. Now we would have two translators.

Noel's arrival under separate circumstances from the other three of us on the U.S. team was suggestive of his stance with regard to the project. Ann reflected once that he always seemed to be "thinking on a track of his own." This meant that he sometimes separated himself from the team. He'd returned to Ethiopia with a special aim to monitor the camp's experiment at raising fish in the long ponds that the first team had dug.

Noel had been a violist in the Stockholm Symphony and had owned a violin repair shop in Pittsburgh. Now he had changed careers and was keen on working in Ethiopian agriculture. When he arrived that morning, I had no way of anticipating what I came to feel later: the old violin he had felt comfortable in bringing to this primitive life was one of the camp's great mollifiers, a soother of the irritations of our group life. Besides his short formal concerts, I came to count on the nights when he would practice violin by candlelight in his tent.

Conversation while we forked and pulled made the time go faster. Sometimes we spoke to the Soviets with the help of Ann or Noel; other times we learned how much halting English they knew. Vladik, who loved to read and would go to law school once he was home in Moscow, loved to talk while he worked. One morning he wanted to discuss parapsychology with Jack. Another morning I talked with him about classical music. We battled at grass roots while humming our favorite Beethoven themes.

One morning Ruslan came to work in the spell of a dream about his grandmother. Ann was working near us, and she translated while he told me his story.

"It's been a long time since I've thought of my grandmother," he said. He was now nearly forty. "What is it? This country makes me think of my childhood." Ruslan's parents were Circassians, both teachers, and they had four sons. His father taught the native language, Circassian, in the local school. Children in Kabardinski, their town, all spoke Circassian, but those like Ruslan, who went to Russian-speaking schools, grew up bilingual. His mother taught in a kindergarten connected to a factory in their town. Ruslan knew how well she treated her pupils, since when his brother went off to a special English-speaking boarding school, Ruslan was jealous, and his parents allowed him to go to his mother's kindergarten to make up for his loss. Ruslan felt his mother made up for the fact that she had no daughters by giving special care to the little girls in her kindergarten.

School was a happy time for Ruslan. When he was in the second grade, his grandmother was widowed. So that she wouldn't have to live alone, his parents gave Ruslan to her. At age seventy she was a hard worker. He remembered her liking to dig and plant in her garden, and as a small boy he liked to work with her. "She kept a clean house, and I had my chores to do in it." He said one of his grandmother's favorite sayings was, "Get up, the neighbor has already taken his cow out to pasture, and you're still sleeping."

As a small boy, Ruslan liked to read, especially fairy tales.

He would go to bed in the same room with his grandmother and when he heard her snore, he would sneak out of bed into the next room and read far into the night.

Like young boys in any school in any country, during the four years Ruslan went to Russian-speaking school, he came to have a crush on a particular classmate. Telling about his boyish obseession now, he stopped and leaned on his garden fork. "I loved her! But another boy in the class loved the same girl. She was pretty! I pressed myself up to her once when I was sitting beside her and my rival got so jealous he dragged me away. If we were so lucky as to go somewhere in a line, we competed to hold her hand."

Ruslan shook his head, and returned to wielding his fork. "She still lives in Kabardinski, and I see her now and wonder, where is her childhood beauty?"

In the fourth grade, when his uncle developed hypertension and severe headaches, Ruslan decided to become a doctor. His grandmother's only son was ill, and Ruslan longed to do something to quiet her fears. "One day I walked to school and nearly forgot where I was going, I was thinking so hard to find a solution for chronic headache. If you could just replace someone's brain, I thought. And as for my uncle, I dreamed of winning the lottery and buying a car to take to him and say, 'Here, it's yours!'"

Ruslan's idyllic school years ended abruptly when, in the fifth grade, he went to a new school where the teachers didn't seem to appreciate his abilities. "They didn't even notice me. There was only one Russian language teacher who could explain things about what we read and make them clear." He forked a clod of earth and mused. "I still think of her fondly."

After eight years of regular school, when Ruslan was sixteen, he entered a local vocational school for doctors. After three-and-a-half years he finished and was considered trained as a medic.

A few months before he completed his medical training, Ruslan's grandmother died. Sad, he stayed on alone in her house, for he felt he was already grown, and to go back to his parents' home would be to return to his childhood. As he lived in her house he came to feel it was his, filled as it was with the presence of his grandmother.

Ruslan finished his story with the account of the death of his grandmother. When he stopped speaking, I went on working feeling a kind of "grandmother kinship" with this Circassian man. Twenty years before Ruslan had gone to live with his grandmother, my grandmother had lived with our family. None of the adults in our family got along with her, but I was a child and she loved me specially. She took me with her on her shopping trips, took me to my first movie, and taught me how to bake apple pie. Often I have wondered how much of my self-esteem came from a kind of early assurance I had: "If no one else does, Gramma loves me!"

By the time we had decided that Jon Jeavon's book on growing vegetables organically was a bible for us, had constructed a sample compost pile, and were becoming oriented to life in camp, it was time for Fred and Pam to leave. Fred took Jack around camp to show him some of the construction jobs which a volunteer needed to initiate. Jack had already begun to carve sticks and attach them to brace our wobbly dining chairs. Fred had sensed that, like himself, Jack was fonder of building than digging, and he assured him that many projects awaited anyone innovative at small construction projects. Gitachew, the buyer for the project, was the person to whom Jack should apply for materials.

The kitchen, in particular, needed shelves and waist-high work space to make life easier for the cooks. The staff in the kitchen was becoming more important to us as camp life developed. The head cook, who lived in a tent in camp with us, was a handsome woman named Edil. She proved to be an expert at cooking something interesting out of next to nothing. A beautiful young girl named Bizunesh helped her with the serving, washing up and vegetable preparation. In addition, Jufari came in each day from Godino. She made all our *injeera*, the bread for our Ethiopian-style meals. About every three days Jufari squatted before a small wood fire in a protected spot and produced about thirty injeera, enough to feed the crew of us for several meals. From a hollow gourd she poured out the fermented dough onto a round twenty-four-inch iron placed over the fire. I liked to watch the long thin stream of dough go onto the iron in a pinwheel and gradually spread out to cook into a flat pancake. Making injeera is a skill most Ethiopian women acquire. Jufari made an art of it.

The Baumans' departure called forth a rash of goodbye ceremonies, especially from the cooks. The day before they left, a tethered goat grazed on the sparse grass near the kitchen shack. That night we ate him. The cooks roasted the bulk of him over a large bonfire. We even sampled his stewed innards, well disguised with red pepper. Considerable chewing is required to eat a roasted Ethiopian goat. No wonder there are so few Ethiopians with fat cheeks.

On the morning of the Baumans' departure, the camp was subdued and sad. For breakfast the cooks had laid out bulgur cereal, tea, oranges, and popcorn. Edil had also baked a cake over the open fire in a large covered frying pan with burning coals piled on its cover. As a special farewell, the ordinary breakfast coffee was served ceremoniously. It came in small cups which nested in green grass on a tray.

The van stood loaded and waiting for Fred and Pam in the middle of camp. Just before it pulled off, a cluster of Ethiopians who had worked with the Baumans in the fields and in the kitchen gathered about the van, wet-eyed. The cooks hugged the Baumans goodbye, then clung to each other, quietly sobbing. It was the end of a brief, good era. It did not matter that there were other faranjis to take the Baumans' places. These were special, well-loved people, and their departure left a huge void. I was uneasy about how well our novice team would fill it.

5.
I Like Humanity—
It's People I Can't Stand!

LIVING communally, even in ideal circumstances, creates irritations. Living communally with a strange and sparse diet, cement latrines, one cold-water gravity shower, hard physical work to do, and no common mother tongue is a setup for struggle.

Ploughshares idealistically aimed to demonstrate a cooperative world in microcosm, one in which widely variant nationals become a close-knit group and work together in harmony. But our team's foreign situation exacerbated the clashes of our diverse temperaments. Stubbornly, the group seemed to resist becoming close-knit.

Each of the thirteen of us had come to this Ethiopian village for a different reason. Our Ethiopian teammates were doing this work because it was their living. Each of them had training in agriculture and had used it in other areas at other jobs. They had come to this FSO job because it was further experience for them, because of the religious motivation of their fellow Ethiopians on the job, and because it paid—their salaries ranged around $150.00 a month plus room and board. Their aims were idealistic—to help their fellow Ethiopian villagers use agriculture to become more self-reliant—but basically, they were in camp as a means of earning their living.

The Soviets had applied to and been selected by the Soviet Peace Fund to come to work in Ethiopia on an "expenses paid" vacation of sorts. They were given a small stipend for spending money and appeared to use it to "party" on their forays out of camp. Except for Ruslan, they seemed to care only incidentally about the humanitarian aims of the project. The trip was a travel adventure for them.

Ann and Jack and I had paid our own airfare and room and board to come and work, and out of that total sum we were paid back spending money equal to what the Soviets were given. Noel had come on his own, was only barely able to pay FSO for his room and board, and had next to no money left over for spending. Each of us from the U.S. had come on a kind of adventure, but we also hoped our work would count. If we weren't quite hoping for brownie points in heaven, we did hope the work we did would add to our humanitarian views of ourselves.

With such diverse reasons for being in camp, how could our team manifest a common purpose?

Three languages splintered our communication. Since all of us came and went in camp, we were seldom all together for meals, but when we were, English, Russian and Amharic divided our conversations. Not one of us understood all three languages. The Ethiopians all had good English and could be counted on to understand what was said to them in that language. Of the four Soviets, only Olga was helpful translating from English into Russian, and that was only at the end of our stay, after her ear had become more adept at discerning English sounds.

Vladik studied and practiced earnestly. He longed to communicate using English, but youth's hesitancy and ambition made him shy of making mistakes. Sergei spoke only Russian and usually opened his mouth, according to those who understood him, only to pontificate or to complain. Ruslan, with no more than twenty words of either Amharic or English, was our camp's great communicator. Masterfully, he found non-verbal ways to communicate. His weight-lifter's energy helped him relate to his patients, those with whom he shoveled, and even the village children.

Ann and Noel both spoke fluent Russian and took turns translating for both Ethiopians and Americans. Noel learned the Amharic alphabet—no mean task, since Amharic script looks to the casual observer like so many gorgeous hieroglyphics. At twenty-five, Ann had already lived abroad twice and was a natural at languages. With her math professor father, the family had lived in France for a year when Ann was fourteen. The school she attended had children from every country, so that on the playground she had heard a polyglot of languages. Only one woman at the school spoke enough languages to draw the children together, and Ann found that woman's skill so remarkable that she decided at fourteen to try to emulate it. That year she became fluent in French, and later, when she attended Stanford, she studied Russian and practiced her leadership skills as a dormitory counselor. When Ann graduated from Stanford she went with two American newspaper correspondents to Moscow as a live-in babysitter for their two small children. That year, using Russian, Ann trained her ear and tongue. She was also actively curious about Amharic, and we watched her go about learning to speak a language from the ground up. She practiced phrases constantly, and pleased her Amharic-speaking friends by learning their songs. Her unique communicative urge made the Ethiopians love her.

Jack and I both found our minds rusty and "sot in their ways" when it came to languages. Since we were fluent only in English and Turkish, often when we wanted to use an Amharic word, a Turkish word came to mind. From steady use in the village I recognized Amharic words like "carrot,""cabbage," and "beet," and purposely learned Amharic phrases like "well done," "good job" and "no problem." Phrases for praise were useful in our work.

I comforted myself by thinking that at Godino school my students learned more when I spoke no Amharic. Only rarely did I ask the sixth grade teacher I helped to translate something I had said. We were working two ways: to train the student's ears to English sounds, and to get those young tongues twisted around my phrases for good pronunciation. Their teacher's quiet voice was inadequate as a model for pronunciation. Her English words came out soft and fuzzy with the lyrical quality Amharic sounds have, but she was not always easy to understand.

Our Ethiopians didn't expect to like the Soviets. The Soviet Union's influence in Ethiopia since 1974, when Ethiopian Marxist forces began to dominate the country's government, has been strong. Because so many Soviets based in Ethiopia are military personnel acting as advisers, they have a reputation for being imperious and superior. At one of our earliest group meetings the Soviets' behavior was true to the Ethiopians' expectations. Ruslan, Sergei, and Vladik all demanded that we must have more meat in our diet. In fact, they wanted to have meat at least once a day. "Men working hard need protein," they claimed. No suggestion that Olga, Ann, Judy, and Asellefech might need meat, too.

Most often we ate Ethiopian-style at our camp's main midday meal. The cooks served rolls of injeera and about four varied sauces or *wat*. Lentils, cabbage, our garden's carrots and beets, sometimes ground meat—all were cooked either in combination or separately in a sauce with onions, oil, and red pepper. At the table, we took a roll of the injeera, opened it out on our plate, partially covered it with two or three of the sauces, tore a piece from the bread, and used it to pick up the wat with our fingers. The cooks, knowing the foreigners could not tolerate the red pepper that Ethiopians liked, often made two bowls of each wat, one less spicy than the other.

The Soviet men's demands for meat once a day put Gitachew on the defensive. He protested that we had no refrigeration and that meat was only rarely available in the village. With the gas shortage and the van in Addis most of the time, he could not get to Debra Zeit every day to procure meat, even if we could afford it. Our best bet was to buy goats and chickens alive and butcher them, but that was expensive.

Belay, in response, repeated that the camp budget did not allow for meat every day. Noel reminded the team that we were eating much better already than the food-for-work workers alongside whom we worked, and this disparity upset him. Ann said nothing, making no issue of the fact that she was a vegetarian. She didn't need to; we knew she didn't eat meat. Jack and I both expressed ourselves as content with the diet the way it was. I saw that I would probably shed some pounds, and I was delighted. Asellefech, Senbet, and Beriso were dead silent.

At length, when everyone who felt so inclined had spoken, Ruslan leaned his folded arms on the table and spoke as if from the heights at the end of the table. "Meat is essential," he said in emphatic Russian. "If the camp buyer can't get it for us, I will go to the Soviet air base in Debra Zeit and see what meat and fish in cans I can buy with my own money."

So it was that in the early days of camp, stew meat, sardines, and mackerel began to appear at our table in jaggedly opened tin cans. The evening meal came at an hour when Edil, our cook, was tired after putting her main energy into the midday meal. At night she often served a macaroni and fish soup (with fish skin and bones). The cans of meat helped silence the Soviets' complaints. Vladik liked to make borscht for the evening meal, and we grew all the vegetable ingredients for it. He refused to make it, however, if there was no meat.

In late March, at the end of our three-month stay, financial problems in the Soviet Union meant that Soviet bases were expected to pull out and did not re-supply themselves. There was no meat available for our teammates to buy, but by that time they were more resigned to our spare diet.

The divergence of the ways in which the U.S. and Soviet teams had been selected affected the way we looked at the camp's work. Since part of the Soviets' reason for coming was to see another country and have a vacation away from the Soviet Union, they didn't see our agricultural work as vital. Except for Ruslan, working with villagers did not appear to take priority.

As the weeks went on in camp, Ann began to wish she did not understand Russian. She grew tired of hearing Sergei's ubiquitous complaints. In the early weeks of camp, he influenced Olga to adopt his work patterns and we came to think of both of them as "goof offs." Once, when I heard Sergei boast about how he learned to work hard from his parents, I asked him how he accounted for the fact he didn't work hard in camp. "This work isn't important," he said.

Jack's and my work with Sergei and Vladik continued to provide contradictions. For instance, the officials of the Soviet embassy were more active in supporting our camp life and in visiting us than were those of the U.S. embassy, and one Saturday afternoon, a carload of Soviets arrived while Jack was working on a mud brick "injeera office" in which our cook, Jufari, could cook her huge flat pancakes. The Soviets were still sitting around the table drinking the vodka the officials had brought when Jack and I came to a stopping place and joined them. Our teammates had left the table, but Sergei was still there, being more willing to continue drinking than the others. When we arrived, Sergei grabbed the bottle with a flourish and began pouring us vodka. He let me demur and take tea. Then he proposed a toast and we raised our glasses. What would it be? "To Jack and Judy," he said. "I am glad to have come and met them because they are optimists." The Soviet official beamed at us as he translated. I wished Ann had been there. We had caught Sergei in a rare moment when he had no complaint.

Vladik enjoyed physical work partly because it was body building. Often he exercized by lying on the ground and lifting large stones. Occasionally he staged contests with other food-for-work young men to see who could lift the biggest stone.

Since they could converse slowly, Vladik made chances to work with Jack on the heavy digging projects. Jack has a perpetual philosophical bent and expressed interest in Russian history, to which Vladik was eager to respond. Work went faster with halting chats. Later, as we became closer to Vladik, he became protective of us. If the physical work was hot and strenuous, Vladik tried to make Jack stop early. Once, when he knew Jack had strained his back working, Vladik asked permission first and afterward came to give Jack a massage.

Willy-nilly, our interest in Russian history grew when Vladik came to massage Jack's back. He knew that we retreated out of the sun to lie on our beds and swat flies during the hottest part of the day just after lunch. The first time he came, while he rubbed Jack's back with his strong hands, he told us a story from the White Russian struggle against the Red Russians. A great way to practice his English! We invited him to come again. The next time he came to our tent with a Russian history book and a Russian-English dictionary tucked under his arm for a highly animated rest time. He perched on the end of our shoved-together beds, and began: "Today I want tell you about the White Russian General Kornilov," he said. Then, in halting English, he told us of how that General had organized a regiment to fight the Red Soviets. "His regiment had 4,000 at the start, mostly officers. By accident, shell killed General. His army demoralized. Only 1,600 left. They buried him and retreated. The Reds came—" here he looked for the word in his dictionary, "disinterred him, and burned his body. Brutal! They did savage things."

We all shook our heads thinking of the blood and betrayal. We came to be fond of Vladik and saw it as a pity that neither for work, nor with other people, did he appear to make an equal effort. His knowledge impressed us, and his clear favoritism for the White Russians struck us as bold. Once, when Jack and I walked a kilometer down the road to signal the turn-off for friends coming from Addis, Vladik walked with us and told history stories while we waited. Our friends were delayed, and we decided finally that Jack should stay to wait, and Vladik and I would walk back for lunch. He insisted on my taking his arm and holding my umbrella to shield the two of us from the sun. I arrived back in camp with a sleeve wet from his perspiration. In our tent, changing my blouse, I found myself touched by the odor of Vladik's protective exertions.

Ruslan also made chances to work with Jack, both in heavy physical labor, and in his informal medical clinics. He often called Jack to puzzle with him over some medical diagnosis. Those consultation sessions must have seemed odd to the villagers—two doctors who had to wait for translation whenever either patient or doctor spoke.

Ruslan lived with Senbet in the tent next to us. Often in the evenings we would hear him. "Ah, ah, my gold friend," he would groan, and we guessed Senbet had made a mistaken chess move. Then, when Senbet made a smart move, we also heard it. Senbet would give a small yip and Ruslan would say, "Ah, my silver friend," implying that Senbet had stepped down a notch in his value when he made a winning move. The camp had one clear example of a Soviet and Ethiopian who were plainly fond of each other.

At the midpoint of our stay, we scheduled a trip to Addis as a morale builder. There was no gasoline to take our scheduled trip to Soderi, but we knew it was essential to take the more possible trip to the capital, and if we all took a break together, it might improve our group life.

While we were in the big city, Olga, Ann, and I persuaded Senbet to meet us and take us to the *mercato*, or market. Late on a Saturday afternoon, Senbet arrived at Balcha from his brother's house. He was reluctantly willing to be our guide. After only one night, I was glad to leave the starkness of Balcha's atmosphere for the crowded Ethiopian streets.

The four of us went out to the street to try to flag a taxi.

Gasoline was short. Senbet could not flag a taxi. Instead the four of us climbed into a covered pickup truck and rode to the heart of the city perched on metal benches facing each other along with other Ethiopians. The truck stopped at the edge of a noisy, confused bazaar, and we all crawled out.

At the mercato merchants line up in myriad open-air stalls and covered cubbyholes to hover over their wares. However, since Ethiopia has a paucity of hard currency, at first glance the mercato confronts visitors with only a collection of cheap trinkets. Parts and essential goods, if Ethiopia manages to import them, are scarce enough that they are not on open display. The tiny shops in the maze usually offer only one kind of item—shoes, jewelry, traditional national dress, contemporary dress, auto parts, yarn, plumbing fixtures, dishes. Together the open stalls and small back rooms present a potpourri of possibility, a kaleidoscope of color.

I wanted to buy several national dresses. In the first shop the owner was clearly impressed by my foreignness. Initially he suggested an exorbitant price for the dress I coveted. The loose white cotton dresses he showed us were exquisitely and brightly embroidered, but too big. I asked for a smaller one. He held up a finger and rushed out the door. When he returned from another shop, two less balloon-like dresses were slung over his arm. Through Senbet, I offered less than his price for the first one, and he feigned disinterest. I stalled, pretending to take a mild interest in several others. After fingering four or five, I made up my mind, indicated two of the dresses I had first looked at, and offered him the price he had quoted for the first dress for the two I wanted. He accepted my offer, and I left the shop with a large paper bundle under my arm. Once we were outside, Senbet told me that the shop owner had offered him, as translator, a cut of the profit. All he had to do was negotiate a sufficiently high price. Senbet's honor had been offended, and he had refused.

After that experience, Senbet had had it. The noise and confusion, coupled with his responsibility for us, had begun to wear on our hesitant guide. "Let's find a taxi, go back to

Balcha," he suggested. But the others still had lists of things to find and buy. We soothed him, we coaxed him, we told him how important he was to us, and at length he was persuaded to stay. He preferred, he said, to come to the mercato alone. He liked to be able to drop into invisibility when he was caught in the confusion of a place like the mercato. In the company of three conspicuous foreigners, he could hardly be anonymous.

We turned a corner and came upon another shop with national dresses. Since Ann was also interested in them, we entered. The embroidery on these dresses was less elaborate, the cotton was of a coarser weave, and the price the more casual shopkeeper quoted was lower. With Senbet's help I bought two more dresses for about eight American dollars each, less than half what I had paid for the others. Ann still could not make up her mind.

We wandered on. When we had bought two kinds of yarn and the plastic shoes our cook Jufari had asked Ann to buy, we moved to the edge of the bustle to find a taxi. Leaving, I recalled that I had seen no baskets. While in Addis, I was approached only once by a man selling baskets as a craft, and that was near a large hotel where foreigners could be found. At the mercato no one appeared to scramble, as I had seen in Turkish markets, to hawk their wares to foreigners. Why should they? They see few tourists. In 1991 only a trickle of foreign travelers were allowed into Ethiopia. Thus, no baskets.

As time went on, Olga became more active in reaching out to her teammates. She liked to knit, and often when the workday was over and her shower taken, she sat on her bed in her tent, knitting. On our trip to the mercato she had bought pink yarn, and at the end of the camp, had made a pink, sleeveless sweater for Asellefech's small daughter.

One of the few Sunday afternoons when most of us were in camp, we sat around the dining table knitting, playing chess, and batting flies. I fished out our pocket atlas and brought it to the table to see where General Kornilov lived in the Caucasus. Our cook Edil spoke no English, and to involve her, I tried to show her on the map where Jack and I lived in the U.S. After indicating Seattle, I wasn't sure I was making myself understood until, as I pointed, Olga piped "Judy's tukel! [mud hut]." We all laughed. Edil, too, gave a hearty guffaw.

To build community and understand each other better, we had certain rituals. At our evening table on the rare nights we were all in camp, we asked our teammates to take turns giving oral autobiographies. Each person had an evening to shine under the stars, but the story I remember best was Beriso's. In his short thirty-six years he had known enough storms to sink thirty-six people, but Beriso's calm telling of his story downplayed all his gales.

"I divide my life into three periods," he began, "my lucky childhood, my unlucky five years in prison as a political prisoner of the Mengistu government, and the mixed years since I left prison. This government still suspects me." Beriso began to speak more rapidly, as if he wanted to gloss over his difficulties getting a job since he'd left prison. Since the government was down on him, he'd needed a job with a private organization if he wanted to be closer to his family. The only job he'd found was in Godino with FSO, still 400 kilometers away from his wife and children.

Then, after he had made sure we understood that he was a family man, Beriso began at the beginning. "Although my mother died a month after I was born, my father's other wife, who had nine children of her own, loved me almost more than her own children . . . I grew up feeling the world loved me." Beriso described how his father had enrolled him in an Adventist missionary-sponsored school when he was nine. "I loved my father so much I refused to eat meals without him, and when he was away, I slept with his clothes. I wanted to bury my nose in the smell of him."

At school Beriso was ambitious. It was so essential to be at the top of his class that a grade of 99 instead of 100 meant, "I cried and disturbed my classmates."

Those antics occurred when he was young. It took settling in and plodding to get through school later. Beriso attended night classes for the ninth and tenth grades so that he was able to work days for the money it took to stay in school. Another way he earned his way through school was to teach sixth- and eighth-grade English in a mission school. In the summers in between the school years, he attended a teacher training institute, and his teacher and student roles became difficult to separate from each other.

Beriso got a lucky break when a Swedish man came to the school looking for two students to employ as forestry nursery supervisors. Beriso won the job and went with the Swede to the eastern part of Ethiopia to work for two years as a nursery technician with the Swedish International Development Agency, using English and Amharic. When the Swedish man with whom he had lived left Ethiopia, the heart went out of that job for Beriso. He entered a Ministry of Agriculture training center, and from that course he emerged as a general agriculture and rural development agent and was employed as an extension agent.

"She lived in the same dormitory, she worked in the institute of home economics, and she was beautiful. Her name was Askale, and I fell in love with her." Even by the table's dark candlelight, Beriso's eyes grew bright as he described how he and Askale had been married and assigned to work in the same locality. Their first child was born in 1978 and they called him "Thanks" or Temasgen. Two other boys, Samsun and Benyemen, followed in succeeding years and in 1982 their last child, Delilah, was born.

When Delilah was three months old, it was the Ethiopian government that tore apart the family's life. The Mingistu government had ordered the peasants to leave their scattered tukels near the land they tilled and gather in villages, and they resisted. The government also distributed chemical fertilizers to the peasants on credit, and when they began to demand payment in much larger percentages than the peasants could manage at once, Beriso took the farmers' side. "I got labeled a 'reactionary,' and a month later they took me off to prison." When he was arrested, he thought he might be gone for three days. He was kept nine months, brought to trial, and sentenced to seven years in prison.

Now the same candlelight made Beriso's face look gaunt as he continued his tale. His years in prison in Addis Ababa had been grueling. "Actually, I can say one good thing about them," he said. "About 75 percent of my fellow prisoners were political prisoners like me. Many of them were from Ethiopia's intelligentsia and had held important educational posts before their emprisonment." Eleven months after the greatest wave of repression, the prison opened a school for grades six through twelve, with a big library and a prisoner as principal. A sympathetic prison administrator knew what they were doing and shut his eyes to the fact that the school was against prison regulations.

It was an odd school in which Beriso was both teacher and student. He taught sixth- and eighth-grade English and studied two years of accounting. The school offered courses in every subject for which they had prisoner teachers, including auto mechanics, health education, purchasing, wood technology, and agriculture, especially horticulture.

While he was in prison, Beriso's wife, Askale, worked for the Ministry of Agriculture in a town where the children couldn't go to school. With some effort she managed a transfer to a town where they could attend school, and the three boys, regardless of their various ages, were all enrolled in first grade.

Later I asked Beriso to describe his three sons. He said they were all doing well in school, and the oldest was at the top of his class. "I don't know why, but there is something special for me about my second son. Perhaps it's because people have told me that this son is like my mother. He doesn't push himself with other people; he's self-effacing and humble." He spoke of Delilah and grinned. "She's nine and in school, and she's beautiful like her mother."

When Beriso had served five years in prison he was

released for good behavior, but the government was still "down" on him. The only job he found open to him was in the Ministry of Coffee and Tea in western Ethiopia, a long way from his family's home. Necessity made him take it. He worked there two years and then resigned to try to find work closer to home. His work in Godino at our camp was closer, but still he could see his family only once every three to six months.

I listened with a sense of disbelief. Beriso told his story with all its setbacks without a scrap of bitterness. His stoicism put me in awe. I had seen him agitated only once, on another night at the supper table, when all our Ethiopian teammates were asked "What would you do for your country if you were leading it?" To answer that question he had raised his voice. "I'd give them freedom. Freedom! Freedom!" he said with an animation I'd seldom seen in him.

With all the struggles our group had in becoming a group, it may have been Beriso who helped most to make us appreciate each other. Was it because we all admired him? Even-tempered, cheerful persons like him are rare. When others waffled, were moody, or disorganized, "Beri" stayed decisive and instructive. His perceptions about people and about the work could always be trusted. His efficiency in a country where doing anything is always more difficult than in the U.S. made him even more remarkable to me. Given the tensions of international living situations, Beriso's equilibrium was amazing.

So it was that our short-lived group life developed—in fits and starts. The original FSO plan would have helped build the group by taking us on trips together, but the shortage of gas made trips impossible. The fact that we did not get the three trips promised us, but only one short one on the final weekend, made the Soviets particularly bitter.

To have any group life in camp, we had to be creative in planning for it. Those plans took a certain energy. Occasionally someone asked a provocative question of all of us that kept us huddled around the table talking in the evening until after dark, but those efforts at group exchange became more rare in the last month of camp. Except for the final trip to Soderi, when we all seemed to be trying again, we lost the heart to build the group's life, even if we had had the energy.

6.
From Living "In" to
Working "With" a Village?

THE first team of U.S. and Soviet volunteers had, from October to December, concentrated on their demonstration plot. They aimed to teach bio-intensive organic methods to the "food-for-work" workers, hoping they would influence other villagers.

"Food-for-work" was a phrase we used for the forty or so workers who came to work in our demonstration garden each day. CARE had given us grain and oil to pay these workers. At the same time they were paid to work, they learned the gardening methods we were teaching. However, the second team decided that relying on the FFW folk to introduce new methods to the village was too indirect an approach. Our idea was to move our work and teaching closer to the villagers themselves—into their own garden patches.

But how was this to be done? First, we had to get to know the village and its influential institutions better. Then, using those contacts, we could perhaps move on to individual village farmers.

On our second day in camp, Fred took us to the village medical clinic to meet Negash, its medic, and his family. Negash was not a doctor. Beyond high school he had completed a one-year health assistant's training course to enhance his natural intelligence and astute intuitions. Negash's presence in Godino—his living quarters were at one end of the ancient corrugated-iron building where he saw patients—made that village a medically lucky village.

Every day but Sunday, patients came to Negash's clinic from fifteen nearby villages, either on foot or by horsecart. Whenever he helped or consulted with Negash, Jack was impressed by his diagnostic acumen. The clinic had no medicines, however, other than vaccines and birth control pills. Advice was what Negash gave to patients, and if their case warranted it, he sent them on to the hospital.

That first morning, when we reached the long, dark iron-colored clinic building graced by a few shuttered windows, Negash's five- and seven-year-old sons, Josephus and Elias, ran to meet us. Fred greeted them each in turn as if they expected him to perform a certain ritual. In a gesture that seemed like American roughhouse, he grabbed their small lithe bodies and turned them so that their legs flew in the air, then placed their feet firmly on the ground and hugged them.

On the verandah outside the clinic, we passed several clusters of patients and their families waiting their turn to enter. In the dark waiting room it took some moments for my eyes to adjust and focus. Health posters papered the fluted iron walls. People sat or squatted everywhere on rickety wooden benches. Young men, old women, mothers with runny-eyed children—all looked ill and too exhausted to brush the flies from their faces.

Negash was seeing a patient in an adjoining room behind an open door, and when he heard our voices he left his patient to come out and greet us. A sturdily built, handsome man, he had the bright eyes I saw in so many Ethiopian men. Since he was a medic functioning as a physician, he wore a long white coat. Inviting us in to see his crude examining table, he turned back and rapidly finished with his adult male patient, who was perched on a wobbly chair near a small desk.

The piece of equipment he took most pride in showing us, in spite of the way its motor rattled, was his kerosene-powered refrigerator. Negash explained that the refrigerator helped him preserve the vaccines he had, since he had very few other medications that required refrigeration. The walls here, as in the waiting room, were decorated with health posters, but both rooms were so dark I wondered how any enlightenment could emanate from the dull, colored pictures.

Negash's practice was varied. He often dressed wounds. In case of illness, he made what intuitive, primary diagnoses he could and sent folk either back home with advice and basic treatment or on to the hospital in Debra Zeit for laboratory tests and whatever drugs might be available. Jack's observation, however, was that common drugs like penicillin and sulfas were difficult to come by in Ethiopia.

Negash seemed happy to know that an American and a Soviet doctor waited just across the stream ready to respond to requests for assistance, and for the rest of our time in camp he sent frequent messages and requests for consultation.

The first of these occurred ten days later, when Asellefech and I had arranged to meet a woman at the clinic. Upon arrival, we learned that Negash's wife, Misrak, was ill; when we went to the family's quarters to say hello, we found her curled in her bed in a back room looking very ill indeed. Weakly she asked Asellefech if we had any heart medicine in camp. Asellefech said she didn't know, but we would send one of the doctors back to see her.

As we were leaving, Negash emerged from his clinic to hear what we had suggested. "Send the American doctor," he said flatly. I demurred. In English Asellefech explained to me that Ethiopians just did not like Soviets. I explained to her what she already sensed. It would be difficult to ask Jack to come alone when Ruslan was the doctor whom Jack had said he trusted to do the camp's medical work.

As it turned out, both Ruslan and Jack visited Misrak that afternoon. The decision they reached had both psychiatric and general medical elements. Misrak had no heart problem. She was unhappy, had a digestive tract disorder, and very much wanted the attention which receiving "heart" medicine would give her. Instead, they left her a digestive tract remedy from our camp supplies. The word the next day was that she was better, and henceforth Jack and Ruslan were both established as a helpful support team to Negash.

But our friendship with Negash's family didn't get us very far in introducing better agricultural methods to the village. He and Misrak did make a productive double dig, and when we made them a compost pile they had us place it in clear view of the village path. The idea was that people might ask, "What's that?" and they could explain.

The day we made the pile was a market day, and our construction of the green heap did elicit curiosity and comment from people passing on the path. But the pile's educational properties were short-lived. Misrak's neighbors had chickens. All chickens in Godino range freely; within five days their claws had reduced the compost pile of "ready edibles" to nothing.

Before the Baumans left, Belay took us all to school one morning. Fred had worked in the school's garden patch, and Pam and another woman on the initial team had taught there informally. The Baumans wanted to say goodbye. We wanted to say hello.

We also figured Godino Elementary School—it served some five villages—might be another "way in" to the villages. The first team had prepared several double-dig beds in the school's garden plot. Now the beds lay waiting for seeds.

Some two hundred students attended first through sixth grade in this one-story, U-shaped, cement-block building. It was rumored that the school's director, Aklilu, and the assistant director, Asmara, and the two women teachers spoke English well. One of the six teachers spoke Russian. The school staff taught everything from writing in two scripts—English and Amharic—to reading, arithmetic, gym, and basket weaving. Ethiopians would be shocked to know that in the U.S., when we want to describe an easy, unimportant course, we call it "basket weaving." Ethiopians use baskets for many household purposes, and the courses where students are taught to make them are vital.

The school intrigued all the faranji campers. When we arrived, the nine of us were paraded in and out of each classroom, pausing only long enough to be introduced to the children in the lower grades. In a class of older students we stopped long enough to sing "Dona Nobis Pacem" since Belay wanted the children to connect the words of its title, "Give Us Peace," with us. After our rusty chorus the students sang one of their songs. When their energetic brassy tones put us to shame, I comforted myself by remembering they'd probably never heard a polished western chorus. Besides, nothing seemed to dent the children's eagerness to be around us.

During the visit, Ann and I offered to teach English, suggesting we might be supplemental aids for ear-training and pronunciation. It was agreed that the following week we would start with the fifth and sixth grades, where Ethiopian teachers taught English five periods a week.

Before leaving the school, we wandered out to the garden plot to see what the first team had accomplished. In addition to six long double digs, a long compost pile lay in the hot sun, its decomposition process stalled for lack of moisture. Like every other establishment in the village, the school had no running water, only a large water storage drum. Each day children were assigned to carry large plastic bottles of water from the stream to the school to fill the storage drum. Although students seemed to enjoy being sent from class to bring water, we thought we observed a consensus among the school staff: the work of keeping crops and compost watered in the school's plot might become a worrisome burden. Still, they seemed experimentally curious. Would compost really help? Would vegetables grown in a double-dig bed do better than those grown in an ordinary bed?

Seeds are magic when they germinate. We figured that if feathery carrot tops and healthy red-stemmed beet seedlings graced the school's garden plots, the villagers might conclude that the school led the way in a new agricultural experiment. Carrots, beets, and cabbage that formed heads when it grew were almost unknown in this part of the country. Zeyneb, the agriculture teacher seemed ready to work with us. He knew that the vitamins these crops could bring to the villagers' diet were important and worth the extra work.

On the following Tuesday morning, Ann and I arrived at the school eager to start in the classroom. But something was awry! The school's ordinary routine had been thrown to the hot African winds, and children from age seven to eighteen milled about aimlessly on the playground. Aklilu, the director, was missing, and a huge thorny acacia branch barricade kept all persons out of his office.

Asmara met us and explained. Someone—they suspected young boys—had broken into Aklilu's office over the weekend. Among the items stolen were some expensive European-made soccer balls. Aklilu had gone to Debra Zeit to summon the police. It was not, Asmara regretted, a good time for us to start teaching.

The children, however, flocked around Ann and me and seemed eager to cut short their prolonged recess, file into their dark classrooms, and pay attention to us. When we learned that school was about to cease for a three-week vacation, we were still more eager to start. So, with what the Ethiopians probably viewed as typical American pushiness, I urged Asmara to let us begin. We'd decided to do some songs and simple pronunciation drills on phrases the students already knew: How are you? What is your name? Where are you from?

Asmara gave in. I went with Zellekech into the cement-block classroom. The white-toothed smiles and glowing faces of forty-five sixth-graders, from twelve to nineteen years old, greeted me. Their age range illustrated the fact that children in Ethiopia enter school at various points in their childhood, whenever their families feel able to send them.

"Repeat after me," I began, and twelve girls and thirty-three boys became a chorus mimicking my every syllable. The older boys in the back were reticent. The younger children in front nearly shouted.

When we switched to a song, I discovered they already knew the words to "Kumbaya." (What makes that song African is its Swahili title, which means even less to Ethiopians than to Westerners.) They had learned the tune wrong. I drilled them on singing it clearly and slowly. Again, the energetic, brassy quality of their voices charmed me.

Since the song wasn't new to them, I decided to pep it up. "When you sing 'Someone's laughing, Lord,' laugh!" I instructed. They tittered. "On 'Someone's dancing, Lord,' shake your shoulders," I told them.

I'm not sure if their nervous giggles were due to their own attempts or to my ridiculous mimicking of Ethiopian dancers shaking their shoulders. But it seemed a good start. Their hilarity was respectful, and it made the cement-block building seem less dingy. Ann had an equally eager response in the fifth grade that morning. We were glad we had pushed to begin.

Our classes ended just ahead of the lunch break. We left the school to walk the kilometer or so back to our camp, and a host of children walked with us. The little ones scrambled to take turns holding our hands. The older ones walked beside us, working their way close in turns to tell us their names and ask questions: "Where do you live?" "In Godino." "How old are you?" "I am sixty." Each child's aim seemed to be to somehow possess us for the time he or she walked beside us. Then, one by one, they trailed off to their homes for the noon meal.

Ann and I finished our walk across the stream to camp slowly in the hottest noonday sun. It didn't matter that we might not be doing much agriculture at the Godino school.

Our contacts with the children were rewarding enough in themselves.

Another attempt to become more familiar with our village neighbors took place through the village headmen. One late afternoon Asellefech and I arrived back in camp exceptionally hungry. We were about to go to supper without waiting to take our cold shower, when Belay told us supper would be delayed. The headmen from Godino and Gowa—two or three from each village—had been invited to join us for an Ethiopian-style meal. The hour had been set for six o'clock. We would have to wait until they appeared.

In addition to our empty stomachs there was another problem: if dinner was late, dark would fall and we would have to light the table somehow. It was decided we would squander some of our carefully hoarded gasoline to power the noisy Soviet generator. I would have preferred candlelight to the one bare light bulb over the table and the loud clatter of the generator. But electricity would impress the Ethiopians.

At six-thirty, Jack and I went to the table. Sitting there with Belay were the number-one man of Gowa, a stocky, solid-faced, bare-headed man of about forty, and a second man wearing a turban and white woven cotton shawl—priestly garb. After introductions I found myself gazing at the beautiful face of the priest. The white turban wrapped about his head set off his aquiline features. He had high cheek bones and expressive eyes, and his gentle manner fascinated me.

We spoke casually with Belay's translation, while we waited for the other campers to gather. Gowa's headman apologized for not meeting our team upon its arrival, as they had done when the first team arrived. He said he hoped to make up for his lack of courtesy by supporting us in any way we needed while we were in camp.

We waited until seven. When the Godino headman, who

lived just across the path from us, had still not arrived, Wandosun brought the food and we began to eat.

We were well into the meal when we heard gunshots followed by shouting. Wandosun bolted out from the kitchen toward the field. He returned with the report that Doctor Ruslan was needed.

In the midst of the confusion, the Godino headmen finally arrived. Not knowing, as yet, what had happened, I somehow associated their arrival with the assault, and became uneasy when the Godino "second man" stalked into camp with a rifle slung over his shoulder. He was seated at the table next to me. The cooks rushed about to bring more food, and we all settled in to eat again. I took more wat and injeera. Eating not a foot away from an up-ended, loaded rifle, I tried to at least appear calm!

When everyone finished eating, Belay rose, made introductions, and invited comments. The leader from Gowa welcomed us warmly. He was fortunate, he said, to be associated with campers from the two richest nations in the world. Not one word was said about our agricultural aims.

Representing Godino, the number-two man stood and shifted his rifle. "We expect a lot from you," he declared, "The government has promised us help with its villagization plan, but they haven't kept their promises." I understood no words until Belay translated, but the man's angry tone was immediately clear. "Godino has very few intelligentsia because there is no light to study at night. We want you to help us get electricity in the village, but all we have seen so far is a few vegetable gardens." So much for the understanding and support we could expect from Godino's headmen.

Nevertheless, I was sympathetic to the Godino officials' hopes! I had already decided that of all the things from my western world I lacked in this camp, electricity was the commodity I missed most. It seemed a terrible waste of good reading time each evening when I blew my candle out and fell back to sleep between eight and nine o'clock.

An awkward silence fell. Belay suggested the campers

sing. "The words to the first song mean 'Give Us Peace,'" he told them, and we sang an off-key "Dona Nobis Pacem." The men listened stony-faced. Then we sang a rhythmical nonsense song, "Sarasponda." Their dull eyes brightened at this livelier offering.

Ruslan slipped back to the table. Although we were all curious, we waited until the guests left to fall upon him for the story behind the commotion. The incident had nothing to do with the gunshots we had heard. Someone had assaulted one of our camp guards, and he now had a terrible gash on his head. The guard had no idea who had hit him and how his head had become so bloody. He was rumoured to have been drinking, which might account for his amnesia. Ruslan had bandaged his head and sent him home. Later we learned that the guard had had a fight with a fellow guard who had also been drinking, and the younger guard, who had wounded the older man, lost his job the next day.

We wrote off our first contact with the village headmen as a bust. None of us felt we knew Gowa and Godino any better. I, however, would carry about with me the image of the fine-featured, beautiful face of the priest, and the experience of what sitting next to a loaded rifle did to my appetite at dinner.

The incident that gave us our best handle on how to "get into" the village came about two weeks into the project. On her way back from a weekend visit home on a Sunday afternoon, Asellefech, our thirty-one-year-old teammate, accomplished what everyone else couldn't do. Her first job in agriculture had taken place three hundred kilometers from home; while working there she had seen her husband and three children only once every three or four months. This job with FSO in Godino meant a cut in pay, but she could go home for a day almost every weekend.

Returning to camp that particular Sunday, having left the horsecart that had brought her back to Godino, Asellefech happened upon a gathering of several Godino women and paused to join them and listen. When she could enter in, she introduced herself and made a proposal: if they were willing to do double digs on the land around their tukels, our project would give them carrot, beet root, and cabbage seeds and help them to plant and raise them. Two of the women expressed a vague interest.

This was our foothold, Asellefech decided, and arranged to meet one of them the next day at the village medical clinic, a location everyone knew. I felt proud to be teamed up with this tiny woman in her clean khaki jumpsuit over the black blouse she wore for mourning. Asellefech's beauty was connected with her fine features—eyebrows, nose, thin-lipped mouth. The lovely shape of her head was accentuated by her braided hair. When she went home weekends, she usually persuaded a neighbor to renew the myriad tiny braids of her hair, which curved gracefully about her head. She wore a scarf while working, but when her head was bare, her looks were striking.

When we reached the village clinic that next morning, an empty horsecart waited at the entrance to the yard. We were told it was for one very ill man who lay on a mat on the verandah with his wife and another man hovering over him. The lady who had agreed to meet Asellefech was not among the others huddled on the verandah. We would wait.

While we waited, Girme, the village agricultural agent, appeared. His clean, patchless blue shirt with rolled-up sleeves and khaki pants placed him a cut above the other villagers. His sandals had full soles and solid straps in contrast to the worn rubber-tire sandals most village men wore. Word travels mysteriously. Girme had heard we were to start agricultural work with the villagers and had come to offer us his help.

At first he spoke a stream of Amharic, which Asellefech translated for me. Then, observing how slow that form of communication was, he broke into the English he knew well but was shy about using. Eagerly he told us about the large farmers' organization, which had members from three of the area's villages. The Godino woman who had said she'd meet us did not come, and we persuaded a woman who knew her to show us where she lived. Girme went with us. Wode Boru wasn't home. But across the path from her compound, Asellefech caught sight of another woman who had expressed interest, and we called to her.

Dinberie, a twenty-three-year-old woman with long, loose curly hair and an even-featured, beautiful face, came to her gate with her two-and-a-half-year-old daughter, Mekdes, on her arm. The packed earth of her small yard was swept clean in spite of the cow tethered in it. A grape arbor shaded the doorway of her house, and a low mud bench ran around three sides of this shaded arbor. The house itself was made of boards and corrugated iron. It had two rooms and a small window for light. I learned later how rare windows were in village houses. Most houses and tukels had only as much light as came in through their front doors. Dinberie might not be wealthy, I decided, but she was prosperous and hard-working.

Dinberie showed us the spot near her house where she thought a double dig might work. In spite of its partial shade, we decided it was a likely site, since it lay immediately beside the irrigation ditch. At this lower point in the village the ditch was a foot wide, a muddy trough running beside the main path through the village. We measured off a one-by-eight-foot rectangle and stretched a string around its four sides to guide whoever did the digging. We explained that once the bed was dug it was important to keep the soil loose and avoid stepping on it. If the bed was too wide, we cautioned, it would be impossible to work in it without stepping in it.

Girme watched our initial efforts. Then, because he had work to do, he excused himself. Any time, for any help, he repeated, we were to enlist his aid. We finished the measuring at Dinberie's and left soon afterward. If she came to camp that afternoon, we promised, we would lend her a tool to do the double dig.

As we left we saw that her neighbor, Wode, had returned home. In contrast to Dinberie's well-swept order, Wode's courtyard lay littered with straw and dung. A dog growled at us from the entrance, and Asellefech drew back. She might well know African dogs better than I, but her sudden timidity surprised me.

Finally, Wode called her dog off and we entered. That first day Wode wore a short-sleeved forest green dress. It was the same dress she wore each time I saw her during our three months in the village. (I don't know why I noticed that Wode's dress was the same every day. I had only two outfits with me for work: jeans and a cotton tee-shirt and a gray flannel jumpsuit.) We stood outside while Asellefech explained her proposal to Wode and her husband.

Wode was an older woman whose bones in her long face stood out below her black scarf. Her husband, a grisly haired, one-eyed man wearing rubber-tire sandals, cut-offs, a grimy sport coat, and an equally grimy sisal hat, observed us from the doorway of their tukel.

Tukels are the commonest form of dwelling in Godino. They are circular houses made of mud plastered over wood with thatched roofs. Plastered mud partitions sometimes cut the interior in half, but more often partitions are built around the edge of a tukel to make sleeping areas more private. Wode's tukel was dark, since it had no window and relied on light from its door.

Wode did not go with us when her husband took us across the small plot where they were raising healthy-looking sugar cane to an open sunny spot which he invited us to measure for three double digs. We did. He seemed a laid-back sort, but he claimed if we came back two days later, he'd have the beds dug. We agreed to that.

That afternoon Dinberie appeared in camp wearing a magenta polka-dot dress and a yellow-flowered cotton shawl that reached from her head to her waist—clearly dressed for a venture out. Asellefech and I located the tool she had come to borrow and walked back with her to her house.

Dinberie told us she had left school after the fifth grade, married, and with her first husband rented the house where we had met her that morning. The grape arbor over the small courtyard and the six wicker armchairs clearly established her house as a place of privilege compared with other homes in Godino. Across the path, her neighbor Wode was rumoured to be wealthy, but her tukel seemed so dark as to be nearly unlivable, and the scatter of straw, dung, and implements in her courtyard seemed to give her compound an aura of poverty.

Dinberie's spindly-legged seven-year-old boy, Aserat, was waiting for us when we arrived back at her house. At first he slunk behind his mother's skirts, but whenever I looked him straight in the eye, he smiled eagerly. Aserat was born after Dinberie's husband had been kidnapped and taken off to the war front. His father was killed fighting, and never saw his son. He left an attractive widow behind. It was not long before Sisay, a tall young man with bright eyes and a mustache, helped her buy her house and moved in with her. Mekdes, now two-and-a-half years old, was Sisay's child.

African children are not often pampered. Mekdes was. Unlike most of the children in the village, who went barefoot, Mekdes almost always wore blue plastic shoes. Once when she stumbled over the threshold of their house and fell forward, I watched her father rush to pick her up.

Aserat, also, was protective of his half-sister. When we entered the compound one morning, Mekdes's nose was running and Asellefech suggested to Aserat that he wipe it. Swiftly her half-brother took a finger, wiped the mucous from his sister's upper lip, and flipped it off onto the ground, as if he offered his small sister such services every day. Dinberie dressed her daughter for company and holidays in clothes that were no less special because they were second-hand. Mekdes expected to be treated like a princess, and she was.

When we arrived that afternoon, Mekdes had been across the path at Wode's tukel. She often wandered to visit her family's neighbors. We entered the compound and Mekdes ran to pounce upon her mother, demanding milk from her breast. Dinberie did not sit to suckle her heavy two-and-a-half-year-old. Instead she hoisted Mekdes to her chest, pulled her breast up out of the neck of her dress, and, standing, allowed her child to suckle. Dinberie's shawl dropped to the ground in the maneuver, and the tear in her dress's waist-band hung gaping open, showing a large patch of her bare skin. She must have been unconscious of the tear, because when I asked permission to take a photo, she was pleased. I took a close-up, the angle of which cut off her torn garment.

In Dinberie's garden we measured off two other plots for double digs, one for beet seedlings when they were ready to transplant, and one for cabbage seedlings. Then our hostess insisted we rest in two of the wicker chairs in her living room while she served us a delicacy, fermented milk. Dinberie brought the milk in tall glasses from behind a cur-tained-off room that must have served for food storage and sleeping. The beverage had the consistency of watery cot-tage cheese, and tasted like sour yogurt. Asellefech accepted the red pepper Dinberie offered us to put in the milk. I tried it plain. Bovine tuberculosis is common in the Godino area, and in accepting this drink, I was aware of the risk inherent in unboiled milk. It was probably not boiled, but our hostess considered it a rare delicacy. I reassured myself by recalling Dinberie's healthy-looking cow. I had seen the animal teth-ered in the courtyard. What's more, we had had no milk thus far at our camp. I missed it, this tasted good. Slowly, while we spoke of many things, I consumed it all.

Instead of sitting with us, Dinberie stood beside the cur-tain watching us drink. She gave Mekdes a small glass, and the child sat on a low stool opposite us to drink hers. Forgetting how rare cutlery is in Ethiopian households, I asked for a spoon to help me get at the thicker clabber in the bottom of my glass. Dinberie hunted out a beaten-up soup-sized spoon and offered it to me. Mekdes decided she had to have what I had, and demanded a spoon.

When her milk was almost gone, Mekdes dramatically tipped her glass and it spilled out onto the packed earth floor. Her mother simply lifted Mekdes from her position near the spilt milk, took a rag to sop up that part of the milk which had not soaked into the dirt, and casually continued to speak with us. She did not scold or fuss. She simply ignored the child's bid for attention.

Perched on a table in one corner of the room were frames with family photos. When we asked about them, Dinberie identified a photo of her first husband and of her second "husband" (we learned later that she had not formally married Sisay). A postcard stuck to the mud wall showing a couple on a palm-infested South Sea island turned out to be a picture she had found and put up only because she liked it.

Dinberie estimated that they could have only one double dig done by the following Monday, since Sisay was in the eleventh grade at the high school in Debra Zeit and came home only on weekends. She would help, she said, but it was Sisay's strength that would actually result in a deeply dug, well-prepared bed. We agreed to come back with seeds the following Monday.

"Do you think that milk was boiled?" I asked Asellefech on the way home.

"No," she said, "they put the fresh milk to set and add fermented milk to start the fermentation process, but they don't boil it."

Asellefech, a trained agricultural worker, knew that boiling made the milk safe, and she became concerned herself. We both knew that if tuberculosis bacteria lay hidden in it, those effects would be a long time in appearing, but if ordinary digestive tract disruption were going to result, it would probably happen that night.

The next morning Asellefech asked me if I had felt any ill effects from the milk. I reported that my system had shown only a slight rebellion, and that was a small price to pay for the headway we'd made. We'd taken the first steps from living "in" the village, to working "with" the village.

7.
The Work That Wasn't Work

THE work to build the demonstration garden grew rougher. The double-dig beds needed sand—lots of it. In rural Ethiopia, if you need to improve the makeup of your soil by adding sand, you find a stream bed that has sand and tote a shovel and a bag to the spot. You don't telephone the sand supplier and order a truck load. You have neither a truck nor a telephone. If you're lucky, the stream bed is close to where you need to use the sand. We weren't.

We located a sandy spot about a kilometer from camp whereupon the grueling work began. One afternoon Ruslan, Ann, and I scraped and shoveled on the floor of a dry stream bed for two hours to produce a small pile of sand about four feet across and two and a half feet high. When that work was over, I dragged myself back to camp determined to avoid going again. The work was too hot and dusty. Other campers spelled us the next morning and found a further blow: someone had been snitching sand from the pile we'd made. Quick, bag it and bring it back to camp!

But how to move heavy sand? We had no gas for our huge gas-guzzling Soviet truck. Several of us wanted to use the donkey, but Gitachew and Wandosun were hesitant. "If we make that donkey carry sand," Gitachew said, "he won't carry water." Result: Ruslan and Gitachew, our strongest men, each lugged a heavy sack the kilometer to camp. They arrived exhausted.

The next day we changed our tactics. Beriso assigned several of the food-for-work women to take Sergei, Olga, Ann, and me to another stream bed they knew about. At the new stream bed, we shoveled the sand directly into bags in small quantities. Then we carried it jointly back to camp, one or two persons to a bag. This proved a better way to acquire sand, but it was still hard, hot work. I was protected from heavy carrying by an assignment to guard the pile. I relished the time to myself left alone while the others took their sacks back to the garden plot. Time alone in camp was rare, and here I was in this remote spot beside a low cliff overhanging a dry stream bed.

I found a scrap of shade and sat down on a stone. The buzz of flies filled the stillness. Birds skittered about me. I was free to look for some scrap of beauty in this eroded cliff face. Was I really in Ethiopia? Could it be January? It was winter at home, and here I was, pleasantly hot! Happily, when I finally did lug a sack of sand back to camp, one of the food-for-work women shared the load with me.

Aware that it was the work of sand collection that I was dodging, I felt lucky the following Monday morning to take off on foot for Godino with Asellefech. Dinberie had said she would be ready to plant the carrot seeds we had offered her. We were curious to know if she meant what she said.

When we arrived in that shaded courtyard, we found her husband Sisay waiting with Dinberie to meet us. I had met few other men in the village who were as unselfconsciously attractive as this tall, striking, gentle man of twenty-two. He had put off going to Debra Zeit and school until the following day so that he could be home for the planting. Having used English to study science in school, Sisay understood some of what I said. His complaint that doing a double dig was hard work, and his pride that he had done it, however, took only a few English words to convey. Before we planted, he showed us the rest of his garden, including a young coffee tree.

To plant carrots, we measured six-inch intervals across the ends of the bed and marked the intervals with small sticks. After stretching a string from the small sticks at one end to those at the other, we used it to guide our long stick and draw a furrow in the bed for the seeds.

The next step was to mix a handful of sand with a handful of seeds. From the edge of the bed, one person moved along, reaching over the marked row to drop the seeds while another person walked behind lightly covering the seeds by pinching the soil over them with two fingers. Since it was a "no-no" to walk on the raised bed once it had been prepared, it was a stretch to lean out and plant the rows in the middle. Carrot planting came to be my favorite work. Quick and productive, the seeds germinated in only three or four days.

The sun is so hot in Ethiopia that new seeds require a mulch to cover them. Sisay brought teff straw to mulch the bed before we watered it. Although on some days the irrigation ditch which ran beside their courtyard was dry, there was water in the ditch that day. Sisay planned to dig one more small bed at the end of this carrot bed, and we promised to return and help plant cabbage and beet seeds in that bed. The agreement was that those seedlings, when they could be transplanted, would be used for Sisay and any of his neighbors who chose to do double digs and wanted beet seedlings as well as this new, better cabbage that formed heads.

Once Sisay's carrots were planted, we crossed the path to Wode's tukel. Wode's one-eyed husband marched us out to his garden patch acting as though he had a double-dig bed all ready to plant. He was bluffing. He had done no digging. A soft-spoken neighbor, however, joined us as we stood gazing at his field and asked that we come to look at his space. He too wanted a double dig.

"I was going to put in *geisho*," he said (the plant used for making the local brew, *tala*), "but you folks are good people, and I'd like to take advantage of what you're doing in the village." His compliment invited Asellefech's instructions. Carefully she explained how to dig and prepare the beds, while he stood rubbing his chin. We left after measuring two spaces. He seemed unsure and asked that we come back two days later to show him while he was digging how to dig it properly. But when we went back two days later, he was not at home and had not dug. In fact, we never saw the gentleman again. So much for his enthusiastic talk about the great thing we were offering village farmers! Could we expect farmers to work in reverse proportion to their ballyhoo about how much good we were doing?

There was no lack of work that morning, however. On the way to Dinberie's we had seen that a nineteen-year-old woman, Asnaku, who had been given time off from work in our demonstration garden to dig two long double digs beside her tukel, was ready to plant. One method we used to get double digs going in the village was to release two food-for-work workers, Asnaku and one other, who had especially visible garden plots, to spend several days preparing the soil. We arrived at Asnaku's to find her raking a row some twenty feet long and five feet wide that she had dug twenty-four inches deep without help. Her slight figure belied her strength.

How did it happen, I wondered, that such a lovely delicate-featured girl lived alone and dressed in black? As we began to plant her carrots, Asellefech asked her. She told us she had inherited this tukel and garden plot from her mother, who had died just a year ago. Her husband was at the war front, but she was estranged from him, and it didn't seem out of the ordinary to her that her thirteen-month-old baby lived in another village with a relative. She expected to wear black only for another week or so, after which she would call the priest and he would come to a feast for her friends and family in her tukel, at which time he would conduct a service to mark the end of her year of mourning.

While we worked in this open spot, several village children gathered to watch. As we'd hoped, they were curious.

We enlisted their aid in mulching the carrot bed and bringing water in plastic bottles from the irrigation ditch some thirty feet away. With a deft motion of her wrist and hand, Asnaku managed to sprinkle rather than pour the water onto the beds as it came from the bottle. When we left, the children were still helping her. It would take many bottles to make the soil wet enough to protect the seeds from the hot sun.

Gazu, another teenage food-for-work worker, worked a plot across the path some distance down. On released time he was double-digging a plot that belonged to his eighty-three-year-old grandfather, who was named Tamure, which means "miracle." When we arrived inside Tamure's compound, we found the white-bearded man hunched on the ground beneath a tree, a loom in front of him. Rapidly, he wove a rough, tough cotton fabric on a loom so crude as to make the fabric seem, indeed, the work of a miracle.

Where was his grandson? He gestured to the field where a boy wearing a baseball cap above his cut-offs and faded orange sweatshirt dug vigorously in the hot sun with great strokes of a large pick-like hoe. Gazu's energy struck me also as a kind of miracle. We watched in admiration until he saw us and stopped. We showed him we'd brought the carrot seeds, and the three of us planted them in one of the beds he'd readied.

With three separate carrot beds planted, it was time for lunch. As always, the trek back to camp across the fields at noon was particularly hot. To forget the heat, Asellefech and I told each other stories. That day she called my attention to the fact that, like Asnaku, she'd been wearing black for some months in memory of her brother, and would for a year.

Some months ago her younger brother, the one her mother was closest to and had made sacrifices to educate, had suddenly become ill and died just as he finished his education. Her mother's grief was still so unabated that she had left her husband and come from her home in the south to visit her daughter in Debra Zeit. While Asellefech was gone all week, her mother kept busy and useful, and slowly her grief was being put to rest.

Only one of Asellefech's children was in school all day. The seven-year-old son was sent to Angel School, for which his parents paid the Catholic church one hundred birr initially and twelve birr a month thereafter. With this job Asellefech was able to go home each week to attend the Protestant Church of the Full Gospel. The service had so much singing that Asellefech hummed its songs all through the week. The family's Protestantism did not stand in the way, however, of sending their son to a Catholic school. They simply wanted him to have the best education in English available in Debra Zeit.

One day, after we'd planted seeds in myriad village double digs, Anne, Senbet, Asellefech and I sat at the lunch table under the canvas talking with Noel about our work. One of his questions helped us to see that we were neglecting education for compost. After all, the closest we came to working miracles was in making compost. To work the compost miracle, all we had to do was get villagers to set a natural process in motion so that nature would transform useless vegetable matter and animal waste into inordinately useful nutrients to be put back into the soil. One of our aims was to help village farmers to see that miracle and make use of it. We recognized it was the wrong season of the year to make compost because green vegetable matter was difficult to find anywhere, but we decided it was still important to introduce the idea of compost to the villagers and help them start compost piles.

Noel helped the outreach team work out a brief sheet in English which explained the process and how to make a compost heap. Senbet and Asellefech worked on the translation into Amharic, and copied it off by hand using carbon paper. That gave us something to use each time we persuaded a family to build a compost pile. We could go over the sheet and leave it with them, in case anyone in the family could read.

The next step was to return to each of our farmers and suggest that for their next crop they would want to renew their soil and that compost piles started now would be the best way to do that. Again, our first takers were Sisay and Dinberie.

One Saturday morning, when Sisay was home from school, we made a compost pile beside the beet and cabbage seedlings we'd helped him transplant. He had fenced them with low thorny brush when deep footprints appeared in the soft soil, and some animal—he speculated it was deer—began eating the tender beet sprouts. When we stressed the importance of keeping the pile moist since his compost pile, unfortunately, was a long way from the irrigation ditch, Sisay asked if we could help him purchase a watering can. In camp we had two watering cans to lend when farmers had young seedlings, but Sisay wanted one to keep. Gitachew cautiously agreed to buy him a can the next time he was in Addis, and Sisay slowly collected the 16 birr 40 cents (about $8) to pay the camp back in full.

So it was that when the heavy work in camp stepped up—gathering sand, and digging a water depot to help keep the demonstration compost watered—Senbet, Ann, Asellefech, and I moved more solidly into village outreach work. I felt some kind of special privilege to be able to distance myself from the farm and construction work in camp. The village work was work that didn't feel like work!

Just as we were forming a regular pattern of work in the village, January 19th and the Ephiphany holiday came to accentuate our sense that part of our "work that wasn't work" was to build trust among people in the village. Villagers looked forward to Ephiphany as a time for dancing and singing and playing games while the priests and other elders of the church feasted in special tents set up in an open space just across the stream. We wouldn't have to walk in the hot sun to Mageera. The ritual was that Godino's priests would partake of a feast laid out by the women in the tents, and following their meal, we were told, the priests would emerge in full regalia and form a procession to the church. We could join the villagers who walked after them.

The Soviets chose to go to Debra Zeit to connect with their Soviet friends at the air base. Jack and Noel were both under the weather. They had drunk no dubious milk, but something else had upset their digestive tracts. The Ethiopian men on our team all seemed uninterested and otherwise occupied, and Asellefech, whom I was coming to depend on, had hired a horse-cart to go home that Saturday. For the first time in several years, she could be at home in Debra Zeit for Epiphany.

So, although there was no one to go with us, Ann and I acted on our new confidence: we felt daring enough to go it alone. We knew the main paths of the village and we needed no translator.

Around noon we heard several gunshots. What was happening? More shots! When Belay assured us they were not the sudden onslaught of the rebel war, but calls to celebration, we walked out, jumped from rock to rock to cross the stream, and reached the tent-studded area on the other side.

We approached the crowd timidly and found that, unlike our experiences on other forays into the village, we had acquired a new anonymity. The carnival atmosphere meant no one seemed to notice that our skin was a different color. Clad in holiday finery, the crowd glittered in the sun. Women wore new, bright-colored satin dresses. Young girls wrapped their heads with unfaded scarves. The white shawls the older women wore for this special occasion had not yet been dulled by many washings. Most men and boys wore jackets over their clean shirts, and clean hats. At this celebration, instead of shedding their clothes in the blaring sun, these villagers had piled them on only partly for protection, mostly for display.

We wandered and lingered. Several clusters of young people—adolescent boys, young men, mixed young girls and boys—dotted the open space in which the tents were pitched, with onlookers gaping at their antics. Each of the gatherings sang a separate song and focused either on dancing or on a game. First we melted into the back of a motley circle of young boys brandishing sticks. The sticks—about three feet long and two inches in diameter—clearly were for both aggression and defense. Two boys circled each other warily in the center. When one lunged and threatened with his stick, the whole circle jerked back to escape his aim. This went on for some minutes until one sudden lunge scattered the group. Ann and I jumped with it.

We landed and joined the awe of a gathered group watching two men in their early twenties. They danced facing each other. Their feet moved only slightly compared to their torsos. The shoulders of one of the young dancers in the center shook so rapidly they seemed to whirr like humming-bird wings. I thought of a male bird's display at mating time. At least the energy emanating from his dance set off a shower of sparks inside me! As I moved to other circles, nothing quite matched the excitement of that young man's shaking shoulders.

Another thing that excited me as Ann and I moved about among the gatherings was the way each circle included us as if we belonged, not as if we were displays to be at the center of the circles ourselves. For two hours we commoners milled about singing and dancing in varying circles near the tents while the priestly privileged—rumoured to range from old men to young boys—feasted inside. No one was in a hurry to go anywhere. We outsiders were occupied entertaining ourselves, while the insiders were ritualistically eating injeera and wat.

At last, however, two brocade-dressed priests flanked by two more, carrying elaborately embroidered umbrellas—regalia much like what we had seen in Mageera at the Christmas celebration—emerged from the tents. The celebrating crowd grew sober. The women adjusted their shawls to cover their heads. Men and boys transformed their playing sticks to walking sticks, and the mood of the holiday changed as everyone fell in behind the priests to follow.

Slowly, accompanied by soft drum beats, the priests moved along the village path to the other side of the village—perhaps two kilometers distant—where the church stood.

When Ann and I launched onto the village path behind the other pilgrims, escorts suddenly appeared beside us. Several companions commandeered Ann. They were young men in clean tailored shirts, who approached her as if they hoped to try their English as they walked with her. Or was it her lovely blond hair which drew them?

Asmara, the Godino school's assistant director, and Girme, the village agricultural agent, joined me. They were young, but their professions made it more appropriate for them to accompany me, the older woman. Their English was adequate to converse. It was a long walk, and when they had answered my inquiries about what was to happen, they helped me work my way to just behind the inner circle of the crowd that surrounded the four colorful priests.

The procession paused in the center of the village under one lone tree while four drummers and seven priests provided a chant and bells. Girme and Asmara helped steer me to a spot where I could snap a photo.

Just three days before, the Gulf War had begun. Once we were moving again, Asmara remarked that he considered Saddam Hussein "an evil man." What did I think?

"He is an evil man," I agreed, "but . . . I'm not sure that to go to war against him is the best way to stop him." As our chat continued, I expressed some mild questions about what the U.S. was doing in the Middle East. Most particularly I said I thought the U.S. should leave more of the negotiating to the United Nations.

Asmara was shocked. How could I question my own government's actions? America, according to Asmara, could do no wrong. Moreover, if Asmara himself believed Ethiopia's government acted wrongly, he could never be so open as to say it to a casual acquaintance.

As we neared the church, I looked up ahead. Tall trees and cactus shaded the gate of the church. Just inside the gate, the entire crowd walked around a sacrificed goat lying with its throat cut. The dry earth was drinking the stains of its blood. Ahead of us was the hexagonally shaped church, painted white with a red-yellow-and-green band—the Ethiopian colors—running around its circular exterior. More trees shaded the church. Some of the out-buildings made of corrugated iron looked shabby, but there was nothing dilapidated about this Coptic Christian church itself.

The crowd watched the four brocaded priests circle three times around the six-sided veranda of the church. Their bright umbrellas remained open, although they hardly needed shade under the verandah of the church. We craned our necks to see one priest holding a Coptic cross while he raised his voice to be heard. No microphones here. The crowd was attentive. He finished and called for a short silence. Then men emerged into the crowd carrying the embroidered umbrellas open and upside down. There was an over-flowing pile of paper money in the umbrella that reached us. No wonder the church was so well kept!

On the way home, Negash, the village medic, caught up with Ann and me. Would we stop at his house on our way home for tea? We were delighted.

The wicker armchairs squeaked as we pulled them closer to a small, low wicker table covered with a white embroidered cloth at Negash's living quarters at one end of the clinic building. First we drank tea, which turned out to be a strong concoction flavored with cinnamon. After tea came coffee, served ceremonially, and finally Misrak, Negash's wife, brought scrambled eggs and injeera for picking up the cold eggs. While Misrak was adeptly preparing each course while squatting over a small kerosene puffer on the floor, Bekele, Negash's fifteen-year-old nephew, squatted beside her and made a show of carefully washing the cups and glasses with sudsy water. The medic and his family knew the importance of cleanliness to Westerners!

We sat for some time eating and chatting, for which Negash's halting English was adequate. As the last of the food was served I noticed through a tiny window that the sun was getting low. Still we sat on, feeling at home and in no hurry. Negash reported he'd seen Belay and Senbet pass the house a while back going in the direction of the church. Idly we wondered if they might be looking for us.

At length we started for home, and because it was dusk Negash walked with us as far as the stream. At home we found our teammates alarmed! Belay told us that at holiday time the men of the village drink a good deal, and in fear for two women alone, Senbet and Belay had come out to find us. "But we weren't alone, always someone we knew walked with us," we protested. "And we saw no one drunk, either."

Belay listened to our account of the escorts who had appeared to keep us company and had protected us. And when we described our visit to Negash he knew that that household's hospitality was some of the best in the village. If he wondered at our trusting natures, he said nothing.

I went eagerly to our tent, zipped it open, and flung myself onto my bed to describe to ailing Jack all that had happened. He accepted my enthusiasm with a mildness commensurate with his queasy stomach. "We're beginning to know people," I said. "We're getting in!"

8.
"Faranji Magic"

THE folk of Godino are superstitious. When Dinberie saw an unusually black child on the village path, she thought he might be Satan. Flood is of the devil. Rain comes from God. Villagers pray for a girl child or a boy child and think God gives them what they get. People living close to nature, people living without the technologies that use science to make magic, are more apt to see much that happens in ordinary life as supernatural or magical.

But "faranji magic" is different. For some villagers the oddity of an encountered white skin makes another kind of magic. If light skin could allure village folk, could it also make them more experimental, more willing to try new things? And could we call that spur to action "faranji magic?"

Asellefech's pale caramel-colored skin and work clothes prevented her from being taken for a typical Ethiopian. To work she wore a khaki jumpsuit of a kind village women seldom wear. These differences made certain villagers think of her also as a "faranji," or foreigner.

Young children were the first to show signs of attraction to "faranji magic." Almost every day Asellefech and I walked across a certain open spot in Godino where three paths and two branches of the irrigation ditch met. On days when water rippled in its widened irrigation ditch, that mecca was livelier than when the four-foot-wide ditch was nearly dry and muddy.

Almost every time we walked through this spot, the smaller children who lived near came running. "Faranji!" or "Judeee!" they shrieked as they fell upon us, diving to touch one of our hands. Initially, they tried also for Asellefech's hand. But after a week she grew impatient with the commotion and turned them away. They stopped trying to touch her. I became disenamored by the commotion they made as well, but I was hesitant to turn them off. Was it that primal need to be liked? I adopted another strategy: when they came running, I offered them my hand without looking at them and continued to talk with Asellefech, since we were usually deep in some conversation. Ignoring the children did not daunt them, but I ceased to be bothered. No mysterious power emanated from that touch, but if some child thought his run to slap my pale hand drew "special magic," let him.

Compared to Godino, Debra Zeit is a commercial center of city size. Its main street is lined with shops that look like rows of small, overturned boxes from which goods spill out the open end. Godino itself has no visible shops, but its Tuesday market makes it a village commercial center. Once a week, every Tuesday, an open space at its center is transformed into a market. Men, women, donkeys, and a few children arrive early to spread their wares on the ground and to buy or barter for their particular needs.

Otherwise the only sign of commerce in Godino are poles sporting at their top a jaunty tin cup. These poles spring up each week outside certain houses. The cups are the sign a woman posts if she is prepared to serve the local brew, tala, for that day. Those who venture into her house can buy a cup of "cheer" for ten cents. In the late afternoon a loud noise coming from the open door of any house with a pole and inverted cup reverberates raucously.

Since the crowds coming to market make Tuesdays extra-lucrative for selling home brew, the housewives living clustered around the market area of Godino take turns hoisting their cups on Tuesdays.

At one point during our work in Godino, my "magic" hand was in demand more for comfort than for foreign influence. One morning early in our stay I walked over to Godino to take pictures of market day. By ten o'clock, a settled group of merchants had already gathered.

As I approached the marketplace, a young child dressed only in a grimy striped dress slipped quietly to my side and put his hand in mine. Not one word did he say to me. I could not recall having seen the child before, but his head was shaved, he had what I guessed were male features, and I judged him to be about five.

Together, we stopped to examine the goods of the first woman we came to. Her goods were spread out on bits of cloth on the ground forming a three-by-five-foot square around her. There was a small pile of what looked like dried lentils, a pile of partially dry, or at least wizened, tiny peppers, and a larger pile of some kind of grain. Onions were the woman's only other fresh product. She squatted placidly in the midst of her offerings, speaking from time to time with the woman next to her, who sat in the midst of almost identical offerings. Perhaps five such women had settled themselves in that area of the market. That day there were no other women sellers of food. They registered neither approval nor disapproval when I took their photo. I wondered if they knew what my small black box was for.

With few words and much gesture I inquired of a young boy who appeared before me grinning if there were baskets at the market. He indicated he would go and look for me, and the small boy and I moved toward the lower end of the square, where a large crowd milled around some ten groups of plump gunny-sacks leaning on each other. The sacks were full of grain. Just below that grain area was what I dubbed the donkey parking lot. Some twenty donkeys driven to market loaded with sacks of grain waited there. Now in mid-morning they stood, heads hanging low, backs bare, ready to be driven back home with what remained unsold of the grain they had lugged to market. Their owners loitered near them. Everyone seemed more earnest about talk than about buying or selling. The child paused there with me, his dry palm still ensconced in my sweaty one.

The young lad who had gone to look for baskets located us and gestured me back to where a man displayed a crude woven straw table. On this particular day, this table was as close to a basket as could be found. I saw how hopeful its maker was, and was sorry to disappoint him. I was looking for a finished version of the fine woven baskets I had seen the school children carrying back and forth to school as they worked on them. In the unlikely hope of assuaging the craftsman's dashed expectations, I snapped his picture.

I spent perhaps fifteen minutes at the market, dropping the child's hand only to take photos. When I walked back to the path which would take me home, the child went with me. He must have walked a good block out of the market holding my hand until, wordlessly, he slipped his hand from mine and turned back.

Could "faranji magic" help entice curious people into planting new seeds and using new methods?

While we were working at Dinberie's one morning, a neighbor woman named Kenani arrived to express interest in a double dig. Would we come measure for two beds at her house? In spite of the wisps of gray hair that emerged from under her head scarf, Kenani had bright eyes and a lively manner. Almost every time we saw her after that initial day she wore the same dirty dress, cream color with huge pink and green flowers, worn thin at every seam.

The following morning—mornings were always fresh and bright, and this one was already hot—we launched out toward Kenani's tukel. To shorten our route we crossed the stream at a lower point than usual and trekked over the open fields from which the teff crop had been harvested.

Kenani's courtyard was separated from the path by a low, spotty fence, and when we started toward her door a dog jumped up from the dust in front of her tukel to snarl at us. Asellefech drew back. The dog continued to growl, and Asellefech continued to cower until at last Kenani came out to calm the mongrel.

Almost every family in Godino owns a dog—mostly as a watch dog—and they all look like members of the same mongrel breed: a black or brown cross between a police dog and a jackal. None of them have spots, and all have medium-length hair.

Dogs were the only creatures capable of turning Asellefech timid. When she and I first came to the village, dogs steadily barked and snarled at us. If a family had a dog and there was no one to throw a stone and drive the cur away, Asellefech refused to enter their courtyard. Later, when she and I continued to take the same paths through the village, most of the dogs came to know us, and if they snarled I could speak to them soothingly in English and calm them. Only once did a dog rush out and actually threaten to bite us. We were on a new path we happened onto by mistake when he ran out snarling at us. Startled, we ran fast! Fortunately, the dog followed only to the edge of its own compound. Still, it frightened us both so solidly that in the wake of that incident we made certain never to take that path again.

After she had calmed him, Kenani's dog lay quietly beside her tukel while we walked thirty feet or so out to her garden. Kenani showed us the spot where she hoped to do her double digs, and while we measured she began pulling the weeds and dried up tomato plants scattered over the area. Her sixteen-year-old son, Gitachew, whom she called Getu, was due back in a few moments. "He'll do the actual digging!" she promised tentatively, but then added that he seldom did anything his mother asked him to do. "Stay til he comes," she begged. Then she explained her belief that once we measured the plots, if we showed her son how to do the double dig, he would do it for us. "He won't do it for me!" she insisted.

Another instance of "faranji magic"? Getu wasn't the first adolescent in humankind's history to resist anything his mother asked him to do. We'd wait and see.

Getu appeared wearing a torn sweat shirt, cut-offs, and a beat-up canvas hat. Asellefech explained to him how a double dig was done. His mother was right. With bare feet and fierce energy, he began to dig where we had put the strings. When he had loosened the soil in the first three-foot section with his pick and dumped the top twelve inches aside onto a gunny sack, Asellefech and I carried the sack with its load to the end of the bed. The dirt we'd moved would be put back in the bed later when he reached that far end. Kenani, who had no cow, went to scrounge enough manure from her neighbors to enrich the bed. We stayed most of the morning, making odd work for ourselves while Getu worked steadily on the double dig.

We were not alone watching Getu work. Three older men appeared to observe the youth's energy in wonder. One of them said he had heard about FSO on the radio and wanted to see what we did. Suspicious, he asked if FSO wouldn't require part of the crop back at harvest because we had provided the seeds.

Asellefech handled him deftly. "We're only interested," she told him, "in helping farmers learn more productive methods of growing vegetables. If a farmer's willing to do the hard work of preparing a double dig, that's enough payment for us." We left Kenani with a bed some twenty feet long piled with manure-enriched heaps of loose dirt Getu had made ready for raking. "Faranji magic" had worked. We promised to bring a rake back that afternoon.

What about nature's magic? Had Asnaku's seeds, planted four days ago, germinated? Was the mulch holding enough water? As we walked to Asnaku's tukel, we noticed that the two-foot-wide irrigation ditch at this end of the village was dry. A dry ditch meant that the farmers at the top of the village, near the head of the stream, had channeled all the water into their fields and there was none left for the lower fields.

When we arrived, Asnaku had gathered a pile of prickly cactus plants and had started to push their stalks into the ground to root and make a foot-high fence around her raised double-dig bed. The cactus, being a succulent, would flourish in the Godino climate if she merely poked it into the ground. She fenced, Asnaku explained, because her neighbor had several chickens. She saw the birds as her enemy since they might help themselves to carrot seeds and seedlings. An odd enemy, that, I thought as I imagined a scrawny hen's head, its wattle floppy, its beak clamped on a half-inch carrot seedling.

Asnaku was another person with amazing energy. She told us she would be double digging a second bed for beet seedlings even though her released time had run out and she was due to go back to work. We assured her that beet seeds were planted in both Gazu's and Dumbari's gardens and we would have seedlings for her to transplant in about two weeks. Good, she knew Gazu and would be ready.

No magic could work against those chickens, however. Some three weeks later, when the beet seedlings were ready for transplant, her neighbor's chickens had eaten all Asnaku's tiny carrot sprouts. She had learned that to plant beets without fencing was folly, and although we offered to help her, she was discouraged enough that she found no time to do more fencing. Her two double digs remained empty up to the time we left eight weeks later.

That afternoon when we arrived at Kenani's with a rake and carrot seeds, the place seemed oddly silent as it lay baking in the sun. Nearing the tukel we saw an old man sitting outside the door, his head thrust forward turtle-like from the collar of a worn sport coat. He sat utterly still.

"Hello, uncle," Asellefech called softly.

"It's Kenani's husband," she whispered to me, adding that he was blind. Both of us were shy about approaching a stranger who was blind. No dog barked to punctuate the buzzing sound of flies in the stillness of the afternoon, and no one else came from the tukel. We waited. The man didn't answer.

Gently, Asellefech called again, and this time she told him who we were. Straightening from his hunched position, he answered in a hoarse voice. "You were here this morning."

Asellefech moved no closer. "Yes, uncle, is Kenani here?"

"She's at her daughter's." He stretched his neck, as if he were rousing.

"We'll come back tomorrow then," Asellefech said. Where was the dog? The quiet was eerie.

"Yes, come back tomorrow. I hope you people plant our whole garden with vegetables," he called in a louder voice.

We both nodded, forgetting he could not see us, until Asellefech remembered and called, "Yes, we'll work with you!"

As we were leaving, Dinberie saw us and rushed out to catch us. A pink organdy see-through dress made her look like a grimily clad town siren. Alas, a goat had raided her double dig where the carrots were planted. Its soft earth was trampled.

As we followed her, I wondered how many more orderly beds might get messed up by unruly animals that the small boys who herded them could not control.

As we entered Dinberie's compound, two-and-a-half-year-old Mekdes grinned at us before she disappeared inside the house. We inspected the double dig. To lock the barn door after the horse was stolen, Dinberie had barricaded the bed with a thorny acacia branch. Five large cavities—animal footprints—graced the bed. No great calamity. We decided to smooth the holes out, put in a few more seeds, and see what sprouted.

While we were straightening the bed and re-planting, Mekdes came from the house wearing a white ruffled dress, torn and drooping at the waist seam. She toddled to a spot beside the garden bed, stopped, pulled out a ruffle of her dress, and smiled her most tantalizing smile. Because her head was shaved like a boy's (for cleanliness) it was difficult to remember she was a girl, except for moments of vanity like this. We made a fuss over the small vamp and left her beaming.

Having found no one at Kenani's, we had time on our hands, and dropped in at Negash and Misrak's living quarters. After the Ephiphany celebration when we'd had tea with them, Negash had said they would like to try a double dig. Rather than fascination with the foreign it was this family's better-educated judgment that these new methods might yield a richer crop that made them want to work with us.

They owned a field in a choice spot near the head of the stream on the high side of the village. That afternoon Misrak took us there. At one point the stream was some three feet wide and flowing full. When I jumped over it carelessly, my foot landed on grassy mud, and slipped down into the water, and I fell. Alarm! Misrak and Asellefech dove to help me up. Had I hurt myself? No. Actually, my muddy wet jeans felt refreshing. I almost regretted the speed with which they dried in the heat of the day.

Bekele, Negash's nephew, was already at the field when we arrived. Bekele was a sixteen-year-old fifth grader at school. His dignified though dirty suit coat and long pants, coupled with his alert manner, made him seem a cut above many of his schoolmates. We had met him one morning in the village carrying a small three-string instrument he had made. Another time we heard him playing a wooden pipe like a small piccolo. He had taught himself to improvise melodies on both instruments. Because he was on vacation now, he was more available for digging. I was eager to work with him and know him better.

We measured off a bed about twenty feet long, and Bekele began to dig. Misrak had brought a thick, floppy basket for carrying dirt. When Bekele had shoveled a load of dirt onto it, Misrak and I took turns lugging it to the other end. Then, when the loads got heavier, we carried it together, each of us with two hands on one side of the basket. I enjoyed that wordless work with Misrak, a tiny, beautiful woman who understood a bit of English. Working together, we didn't need her English.

Because Misrak's mother had recently died, she wore a black dress that hung limply on her slim figure. She did not like living in this village, and because her education was better, considered herself superior to the people of Godino.

By noon the four of us had prepared enough of the bed so that Bekele could finish it, and that afternoon we planted carrot seeds in it.

Later Asellefech and I went back to Gowa to see some double digs that the previous team had encouraged people to dig. What we found did not bode well for the lasting impact of our work. In three women's gardens we saw lying bare the double digs which had been dug in the rainy season for beets and carrots. They had been harvested but not replanted. Only a few dried-up vegetable plants remained. Most garden plots in Gowa get no water from September to June, depending only on rain. Each woman told us she intended to replant the beds, but not until the rains came in June. Gowa's water comes from an unpiped stream, and families can obtain it only in small quantities after a long walk.

The path to Gowa is long and hot. Before we walked back, Asellefech proposed to introduce me to another woman, Aserati, whom she had met two months earlier with Betty Jane, a member of the previous U.S. team. Gowa is less tree-shaded than Godino. Its houses are arranged in blocks on a grid of straight paths. The paths all seemed alike that morning; we turned down several before we could find Aserati's daughter's tukel.

A grandchild playing in the dooryard saw us and rushed to a second tukel shouting, "faranjis, faranjis!" Aserati, a slim, gray-haired woman whose curly, short-cropped hair was not yet covered that day by a scarf, appeared in her doorway, delighted. Still another foreigner had honored her with a visit.

She invited us in. To seat us, she instructed a child to throw a goatskin over the four-by-twenty-four inch board bench which sat some three inches off the floor of her dark, windowless tukel. Wearing a dark-colored, plain short-sleeved dress, Aserati settled herself on the bed above us and sent the grandchild scurrying off to get her daughter to come and make us coffee. Once my eyes got used to the glare of the light coming in the door, I could make out Aserati's dignified face. The wrinkles were myriad and deep, the features even.

This was one of several occasions when I observed the coffee-making ritual in a village home. A fire was built in a bowl-like, clay stove on the floor. The coffee beans were washed twice in a shallow, curved iron pan before being roasted over a small fire in that same pan. When the beans turned from gray to very dark brown, they were poured into a wooden mortar about eight inches deep. The fire was then given over to the water, which was heated in a blackened clay pitcher with a narrow three-inch spout.

While the water was being heated, the roasted coffee beans were pounded to a powder with a heavy iron pestle. The powdered coffee was then boiled briefly in the pitcher, and sugar added, if the family had any. Before pouring the brew into small handleless cups the size of Chinese teacups, it was allowed to settle. If the hostess had time to anticipate her guests she gathered grass and served the cups on a tray covered with a layer of long, fresh, green grass.

Aserati's daughter, called upon to serve us without advance warning, had lined up three cups on a plain wooden tray without grass. Aserati, perched on her bed like the matriarch she was, drank with us, but her daughter did not sample the coffee she had made.

While the coffee was being prepared, Aserati held her daughter's tiny three-month-old baby, who was fussing from a vaccination the day before. When he was restless, his grandmother jostled him and cooed to him. At one point she handed him to me, judging that I, a grandmother, would enjoy holding a small baby. I did, except that I was worried he would fuss inordinately in the arms of a stranger. By clucking, singing, and rocking the child, who was dressed only in a long cotton shirt without diaper, I managed to keep him from wailing. At one point his mouth nuzzled vainly at my breast. "No milk there, little one," I told him regretfully. Once the coffee was served I could hand him back, feeling I had passed my test. Pronto, his mother put him to sleep by giving him her breast.

Our chat became an exchange of stories between Aserati and me. Aserati's brisk tone rose as she described her married life as a "merchant." Her tukel had been the scene of much coming and going in the village where she had lived before coming to Gowa. ("Merchant," Asellefech told me later, probably meant that she made and sold the local gin from her home.) Aserati's enthusiasm waned as she described her disappointment when her son failed his examinations several times and did not qualify for the University in Addis. (I learned later that he had been our camp guard—the one dismissed for assaulting the older guard.) A mother's fierce loyalty crept into her tone as she described her hope that he could at least become a teacher.

Several years back, Aserati had moved the 25 kilometers to Gowa in order to live beside her daughter. Was it her natural sense of superiority or her veneration for the past that made her insist that the people where she had lived before were "much better than those in Gowa"?

Aserati was much taken with the idea that I had "been blessed" to live with the same husband for thirty-eight years. "You must really love him and be in heaven!" she claimed. "When I married my first husband, I didn't know what marriage was all about. I divorced him quickly." When her next husband died, she married a third. She said she was happy giving birth to her children and being married to her two later husbands, "but now is the best time of my life because I'm living with my son and across the compound from my daughter and I have six grandchildren around me."

On the way home, the image of those three dried-up double digs returned to bother me. "Isn't there something we could help these farmers to plant so that they'd still have something bearing in the dry season?" I asked Asellefech. We decided to check with Belay and Beriso. Perhaps if we were producing enough fruit tree seedlings on the demonstration plot, we could distribute them in Gowa just before the rainy season began.

Their answer was yes. We were growing some tiny fruit trees in special compost and with the proper timing, they could be planted and would flourish in the rain. If the small trees got a good start, they could be kept alive with hand watering throughout the dry season. With the addition of fruit, families might have more income and more variety in their diets the year 'round. Excitedly, we began to make plans to distribute fruit tree seedlings in Gowa at the start of the rainy season. We didn't know the war would ruin those plans.

When we returned to Kenani's, we learned why she had been called to her daughter's house. The daughter had quarreled with her husband. It seemed their cow had produced a calf and the husband had put a rope on the calf to take him off to market to be sold! A struggle ensued when the daughter insisted that they should keep and raise the calf. Kenani was called to mediate, but tempers soared. Finally, the daughter dragged the calf by its rope to her mother's house to stay the night. So the struggle over whether a calf should be kept or sold was a significant domestic quarrel in Godino! How different, I wondered, is that quarrel, from the flaps that send an American woman home to her mother in a huff? Kenani's daughter, being at her mother's, helped us plant the carrot seeds.

Belay came to find us that morning. He had not yet seen

the kind of work we were able to start in the village, and wanted to be able to show some of the double-dig beds to a Dutch donor who was scheduled to arrive. While Belay walked about with us, we told him the story of one of the contact farmers, an older man, who had planned his double dig with us for that week. When we arrived to work with him, he said he could not do the work because his daughter had died. A woman of about thirty, with four young children, she had "high blood pressure" and had been seized by a kind of paralytic stroke from which she never recovered.

Now, when we passed her father's house, there was a huge circus-like canvas tent erected in the old man's courtyard. Belay suggested we go into the tent to express our condolences. Whenever someone died in the village, the family applied to a village cooperative organization requesting that a tent be erected just outside their family home. When this was done, the organization provided chairs to line up inside the tent, ready for the mourners who came to share the grief of the family.

Asellefech and I slipped into rickety chairs just inside the tent, and Belay sat across an aisle from us beside a young man of about thirty who was slouched in his chair. On the other side of the fifteen-by-twenty-foot tent, opposite three rows of some twenty-five chairs, straw tick mattresses with white cotton covers were spread on the floor. Now, three of the older members of the family sat or lay on the mattresses. The grieving father, our potential contact farmer, sat cross-legged on a mattress. Asellefech told me the family probably all slept on the mattresses together for as long as the tent was up. When we were seated a young girl rose from the family area and thrust a basket at us which contained hot roasted sunflower seeds. We took a handful and sat silently chewing them, our heads bowed. An old woman lying on the mattress moaned softly. Belay, when we looked over, was speaking quietly with the young man, who was the dead woman's brother. "We did everything we could, took her to the hospital, everything we could," he told Belay, "but the day she was to die arrived, and we have to accept it." We stayed, sitting silently, for perhaps fifteen minutes, until it seemed acceptable and Belay gave us the signal that we should leave.

At the end of each day when we had worked in the village, Asellefech and I returned weary-limbed but happy. "Faranji magic" seemed to be working. Very soon, however, I began to feel that I was a recipient of a kind of reverse "faranji magic." These villagers were foreigners to me, and their foreignness carried with it a disarming naivete, a compelling simplicity. Working with them added an odd energy to my life. I felt both exhausted and restored at the end of each day.

That evening after the funeral tent there were only nine of us in camp and Vladik made Russian borscht soup. Whenever we asked him to make it, he always claimed to have no interest in cooking his specialty without meat. This time we persuaded him to make it, meat or no meat. Neither was there sour cream. A certain "cook's magic" must have made that borscht disappear.

Few of us were at the table, and the food was good. We felt particularly fond of each other that night; we knew Roba and Belay had struggled that afternoon, without much success, to persuade the Dutch visitor that the project was worthy of a large Foundation gift. In the face of our defeat by the Dutch, we wanted to do something to cheer Belay up. Noel offered us his magic: a violin concert.

We moved chairs to the cement floor of the wash house, planted candles in melted wax on the cement-block wash tubs for light, and prepared for a concert. I held the music for Noel, Beriso held a flashlight to the music, and we all listened spellbound. Noel played jig tunes, Schubert, and much Bach. Playing by candle and flashlight, Noel made magic float out over the clear night air. Bach had never been better.

9.
A Venture into Gowa

FIVE weeks into the project, as the two outreach teams scrambled to find "contact farmers," the village work got a boost. Asellefech and I were in Godino on a Tuesday afternoon just as the weekly market was breaking up. Suddenly a wiry, sharp-faced woman, the President of the Gowa Women's Association, stopped us. She was on her way home with her husband, but had stopped at the Godino medical clinic to persuade Negash, the medic, to come to Gowa on the following day for an eleven o'clock meeting of the Women's Association. He would speak about health. Would we come, too? We could describe to the women the ways in which we could work with them.

Yes. It was a chance we couldn't let slip.

Gowa was different from Godino. Compared to Gowa, Godino had an abundance of community facilities: a school, a medical clinic, and the headquarters of the farmers' association for the surrounding area. Oddly, these advantages seemed to make Godino's people less rather than more community-spirited. Did they take their privilege for granted and become more complacent about village life? Or was it that their leaders were less adept at fostering community? Did they resent the outsiders who arrived to use their school and clinic, buy at their Tuesday market, and urinate in the dust of their village square?

Since by reputation Gowa's farmers were good workers and receptive to new ideas, FSO was eager to expand our contacts in that village. The following day Asellefech and I arrived at the house of Aserati, the woman leader. (It was only a coincidence that the two strong women we knew in Gowa were both named Aserati—one the matriarch, one the childless head of the Women's Association). At a few minutes before eleven, however, she was not ready to go with us to the building where the meeting would be held. Aserati was a forceful woman, but at this moment she seemed particularly casual and in no hurry. Her mother, a wizened figure of some eighty years, held court in a corner of the large room and invited us for coffee. We demurred, figuring it might delay Aserati since she would have been called upon to make it. Instead we sat to chat with the old woman while her daughter flitted about readying herself. This house, more prosperous than others we had been in, had two rooms, a window, a row of wicker chairs for sitting in the larger room, and a cooking stove raised off the floor. An English motto framed on the wall read, "Learn from a wise man and you will become wise."

Once she was ready, Aserati stood by the door and addressed us decisively from across the room. "I want you to make it clear that clothes should not be washed at the top of our stream." Asellefech translated for me. Clearly, Aserati had a hidden agenda for this meeting. "Women wash in the stream and the water comes down filthy!" She shook her head. Did instruction about clean water fit our purposes at this meeting? Negash, the medic, of course, would be speaking about village health matters. He might well include remarks about keeping the water supply clean. Should we? No matter. I decided not to worry. Asellefech could be trusted to work that bit of village politics into her talk if and where she felt it was appropriate.

Two women drifted in to walk with us to the community

building where the meeting would be held, and we left Aserati's house. But from her courtyard's gate, we did not turn toward the women's association meeting place. Instead, we turned toward the edge of the village and walked through it foraging for women to come to the meeting. While we dawdled on the paths between houses with acacia-fenced courtyards, each time Aserati saw a woman—she seemed to know everyone—she stopped to threaten. "You better come to the meeting, or . . . "

"I have a sick child," one woman said.

"My husband is coming home." Another woman hesitated.

After four women had pulled white shawls over their heads and joined us, we arrived nine strong at the windowless corrugated iron building where the meeting would be held. Now the longest wait began. We stood or squatted in the sun outside the building chatting quietly and waiting for more women to gather.

Glancing about I noticed the first woman I'd seen with a tattoo on her chin. Also, I made a note to ask Asellefech if there was any reason why some women wore full scarves rounded across their foreheads and tied at the back, and some older women wrapped scimpy scarves around their heads tied in front.

One woman arrived with a baby slung on her back in a white cotton shawl. We clucked and cooed over the child. Later, the mother withdrew to the shade, squatted, and pulled her breast up and out of her dress to nurse her baby.

A little over half an hour passed before Aserati and two of the other women suggested we wait inside out of the sun. Aserati sat with us at the heavy table in the front of the room. Two other women settled facing us on the front benches. Rows of benches continued into the shadowy back. The windowless room's only light shone in from the door.

Negash had not arrived. Asellefech reviewed with me what she proposed to say. "I'll talk about the vegetable seeds we have and why they're good. Then I'll explain how to do double digs, and I want to tell the women about a new kind of stove that burns more efficiently." Gently I suggested that she simplify her remarks. "Why not deal only with the carrot, beet and cabbage seeds we have, and why it's good to grow them in double digs. Do they understand the importance of a healthy diet?"

"I'll try to help them get that idea," Asellefech decided. But then she had a new idea: I should speak first. If I greeted them in English she would translate. "You can make it clear how we're connected to FSO."

We waited another twenty minutes. Negash finally appeared at the door, and Aserati called in those women who were outside. By this time the group had grown to some fifty or more. They filed in, filling some eight rows of benches. I could see only their white shawls in the back and shadowy reaches of the room.

Aserati introduced us and Asellefech deferred to me. "I've heard the people of Gowa are hard workers," I began. "That's why we are happy to come today. Family Service Organization would like to work with you. . . ." I went on to explain that we hoped to introduce vegetables to their diet for more variety and better health, but I heard Asellefech translate with a sinking feeling. They were so unused to translation that I was a curiosity rather than any semblance of an educator.

I finished and Asellefech continued by telling the women a story I had mentioned to her casually. It was about the time I wanted to prune some fruit trees and Jack didn't share my sense of urgency about the job. When nothing got done, I ignored his indifference, started the job, and Jack's sense of obligation got the better of him and he helped me finish it. Asellefech claimed these women had husbands and sons who might be reluctant to try the new double digs, but that persistence was essential. When Asellefech had described the good uses of vegetables, she moved to the point about clean water. Aserati beamed.

Asellefech finished and asked if there were questions.

One woman rose. "I know it is good to work with these people because my son works in their field and brought home the seeds." There were several other questions about the vegetables before Asellefech put a sign-up sheet out on the table and women began to come forward to have their names recorded. But it was already Negash's turn to speak. Asellefech recognized that her sign-ups were delaying his start and postponed her recording until later.

By this time a cluster of women had gathered about the door, unable to come in. Every bench was full and onlookers were standing at the edges of the dark, packed room. Negash didn't want to start when there were women still outside. It was decided we should move outside and behind the building.

We straggled out to the back, where we filled three sides of a U-shaped courtyard made by three buildings. About thirty curious men joined us, standing to listen at the open end of the courtyard. The women squatted on the ground in three tightly packed rows under the eaves in the shade of the buildings. Aserati, pleased to have attracted such a crowd, asked Asellefech to repeat her remarks so that the men could hear them. The women listened again in the noonday heat, their faces expressionless.

Then, for fifteen dutiful minutes, the crowd heard what Negash chose to say. I picked out enough words to know that he, too, spoke about vegetables. Later Asellefech whispered, "He's talking about birth control pills. He has them at his clinic. He says they should have prenatal care, too." While Negash spoke I counted the house. Standing, sitting, and squatting on every side of the courtyard were 105 people.

When Negash finished, he gave his emphasis to the water issue. Aserati saw her chance and jumped up. "The water flows past our house filthy," she complained. "The health our friend Negash speaks about will be ruined if people go on washing clothes so close to the head of the stream." Her high-pitched, sharp voice was unpleasant. I watched several of the men mutter and shift. One man spoke to support her. Another suggested that a boundary should be established above which no one did any clothes washing.

Another man had a new idea. "The government ought to install a pipe at the source."

Aserati's temper flared. "That's no solution!" she shrieked. "Your wife's just washed the birth clothing of your twelfth child high in the stream."

"You're childless, that's your trouble!" the man fired back. More hot exchanges took place between Aserati and two other men. No other woman spoke. Rage erupted in the crowd, and more men spoke briefly but with emotion. At last there flew calls of "Enough!" and an awkward silence fell.

In the silence another man saw his opportunity. Out from the edge of the crowd came a voice: "We want to build St. Mary's Church in Gowa," he said. "We need your money." Clever man. He may or may not have been a priest, but he saw a crowd gathered and silent and seized his chance.

Once tempers were calmed, Aserati read from the Women's Association ledger book. "Girme Asnake, three birr. Besoonich Berhan, three birr. . . ." In monotonous tones she read name after name, followed by the dues the member had paid the previous year. "Time to pay up again." More demands.

The sun was at mid-sky and hot! Where I sat in the shade, the glare was still bad. I was relieved when Negash broke in to say a few parting words, and Asellefech announced that there were eleven names on the list of persons who said they wanted to work with us. As we rose to leave, I called one phrase in Amharic: *"Amasa genalo,"* which means thank you. The crowd burst spontaneously into enthusiastic applause. Language, I thought. How important it is! I should know more. It's not good enough to use translation. Though Asellefech was adept at translation, I knew then it wasn't right to depend on her so heavily.

We trudged home in the hot sun with Negash, who was

excited about the gathering. "It was special," he said in English.

After Negash left us, Asellefech and I made a plan. We decided to recommend that the outreach team split up. At the moment all four of us were going to both villages. Now, if Ann and Senbet chose, they could follow up on these initial contacts made in Gowa; Asellefech and I would continue to work with the Godino farmers.

Back in camp we looked for Ann and Senbet. How did divided responsibility for the two villages look to them? Ann didn't answer immediately. She was distracted by another tale. During lunch a teen-age girl, one of the food-for-work workers, had run wailing down the road just outside our camp's acacia fence. Our teammates had sent Senbet to find out what had caused so piercing a cry. It seemed that the Gowa village elders had been told by government authorities that they would be carried off to prison if they did not produce eight recruits for the army. The girl's only brother had been seized and taken from the village. He would be given six months of training if he were lucky, and then forced to fight. His family knew he was not likely to come back. Other men had returned only when they were maimed. Most men were killed.

Senbet found the other food-for-work villagers sitting sullen and dejected at their noon break. Who would be taken next? Several of the young men decided to sleep in our demonstration field that night instead of going home. If they couldn't be found, they couldn't be taken. Staying away from home was a risk, however. Parents had been put in prison when their sons could not be found for the military.

During the next days in camp, the atmosphere was tense. Ann, Senbet, Asellefech, and I went to Gowa two days later to follow up with the women whose names we had recorded for work with us. In spite of the Gowa folk's fears for their young men, they remained receptive to working with FSO.

The dread of being taken became clear when we were seated in the front room of one woman's two-room house.

Her healthy young son came in, sat in the corner of his mother's living room, and listened to her plans to grow vegetables. Observing him, I said to our hostess, "You're lucky to have a good strapping son to dig for you." She shrugged. "But I can't ask him to go out in the open to do this digging," she said. "It used to be lucky to have sons, but it isn't now. If you have sons, you know you'll probably lose them to the war."

As we walked about the village that day, the word appeared to have spread, and several more farmers, both men and women, met us on the paths to get on the list to work with us.

The first woman whose home we visited served us hot roasted chickpeas before she told us there would be a delay. Could we wait to work with her until she harvested her onions? Shortly, she would take the onions from the place she wanted to re-dig to prepare it for the new carrot and beet and cabbage seeds.

Two others on the list didn't have water enough nearby to make a double dig worthwhile. One woman had a crippled son and no one to do the double dig. She had put her name on our list, she said, because she wanted to have more contact with us. Still, we came home that day with fifteen new contact farmers in Gowa lined up to do double digs and plant vegetables in the coming days and weeks.

That afternoon a huge CARE truck arrived, piled high with a hundred plump grain bags: pay for the food-for-work workers. When the huge, shiny truck drove through the gate, Jack, Asellefech, Senbet, Vladik, Olga, and I were sitting at the tables under the tarp battling the flies on our afternoon tea break. Suddenly some twelve eager food-for-work men turned up to unload the truck. Pay had appeared. An occasion for a party!

Each wheat bag weighed fifty kilos and had to be carried about twenty-five yards across camp for storage in a small dry shed. We watched while a steady stream of workers ran back and forth, carrying one bag at a time from the truck-bed to the shed. To lug the bags was a chance to show off.

First, each man shifted a huge sack off the truck onto his shoulders and jumped about until it settled into a comfortable position. The younger men trotted off carrying their sacks. Old Arpa walked slowly and deliberately. Two men attempted taking two bags at once, but the weight of that effort brought it to a rapid stop. Too much! Boasting, joshing, stumbling, the unloading became a game. Heavy work grew lighter.

Eight young food-for-work girls finished work at four and joined the men. Several of the girls showed off by lugging, singly, an entire bag. Most of the girls teamed up with another girl to drag the bags hanging low between them. As they sped between the truck and the shed, the slap of their sandals sounded on the ground. It punctuated their laughter.

The girls had arrived late, and by the end were the only ones still carrying sacks from the truck when its flatbed was finally emptied. Were any of the young men and girls showing off because they were eyeing each other as mates? I wasn't close enough to the workers to know. What I knew was that gaiety had lightened everyone's mood. Any excuse to laugh, and these folk snatched it!

Edil, our cook (top), and Arba,
the old man who danced so readily.

Jufari, the woman who made all our injeera *(top). Note the tattoo on her chin. Zeynebe, the boy with the short leg and shriveled foot.*

Bizunesh, one of our cook's helpers (top), and Yalem Zode, another of our cook's helpers after Bizunesh quit.

Godino food-for-work workers.

124

*Ruslan with a dik-dik one of the villagers had brought (top),
and the Coptic Orthodox priests in their procession on
Christmas Day, January 7.*

One of the food-for-work workers with the mold we used for making mud bricks for building tukels.

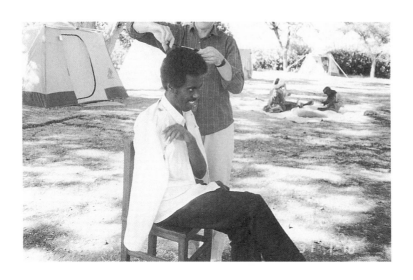

Pam Bauman cuts Belay's hair (top). A group of young village men playing a stick-game at the celebration of Epiphany, January 19.

A first-grade class at Godino School (top). Note the age range.
Akilulu, the school director, is in front of the class.
Below, the young priest Kafalaigne's wife makes coffee for us.
Note how it's served with fresh grass on the tray.

*Aserati, the women's leader in Gowa (top), showing her
pride in her kitchen. Instead of having to squat to cook,
Aserati had a rare waist-high stove.
Below, Sisay, Getu, and Asellefech transplant beet seedlings.*

129

*At the Tuesday market, selling piles of food (top)
and sugar cane (bottom).*

130

Dinberie nursing Mekdes (top). Children's heads are often shaved for cleanliness. Below, Asellefech stands beside the women's tent, which had to be tied up after the storm blew it down.

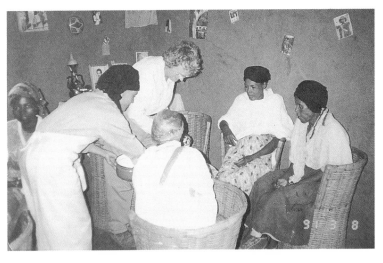

Sisay eats with the women at the party in his home (top).
Note the wall decorations. Below, Asellefech and Judy
serve beet root to Wodu and Zeynash.

132

The women lick the platter clean at the party (top).
The last breakfast at the camp's shaded table before we left.

A woman at the party in Gowa cooking the beet root.

10.
Important:
Forget About Comfort;
Just Stay Healthy

THE tents in Godino were comfortable enough except at certain times: night, when our mattresses became the trampolines for fleas; midday, when, inevitably, the sun turned our tents into ovens; and other daylight hours, when, because we couldn't always make their zippers work to close them, our tents became fly havens. Our tents were our own havens only in the early evening after dinner, when the flies went to bed on the overhead canvas and flashlights or candles had to illuminate what we did. In those evening hours we often read or played chess until our eyes grew tired. Writing was difficult for lack of a hard surface. I can't really say I relished going to bed with the birds, except on those nights when I was so physically weary that crawling into my bed was practically a sensual experience.

Still, the rhythms of our days in Godino had a simple, even quality I came to cherish. I liked the sameness of the work schedule. What gave it variety and interest was the people with whom we worked each day. We kept adding new contact farmers and returned briefly for checks to the ones with whom we'd already planted.

Each morning it became clear whose bed the fleas had invaded by which sheets were hanging on the camp's clothesline. We used flea powder to sprinkle between our sheets, eucalyptus leaves to scatter over our tent floors, scotch tape to pounce upon and squash the fleas, and in the end learned to live with the bites we could not prevent.

Foreigners in Africa most often take precautions against mosquito-born malaria. But high on the Ethiopian plateau, where there is little water in which mosquitoes might breed, we seldom saw the tiny varmints, and the bitter tasting medicine we took faithfully as a preventative to malaria appeared to be unnecessary. (We didn't neglect to take it, however.)

Ethiopia has its own unique pest. As we drove to camp, Fred told us about *mujalis*—an insect like a tick that burrows under the skin, lodges itself like a queen, encysts, and proceeds to lay eggs in human flesh. One becomes aware of hosting a mujali only when the cluster of the tiny pest's eggs grow to about a quarter of an inch across. Since mujalis live on the ground, feet are their main targets. Those who go barefoot or wear sandals without socks have more trouble with them than those who wear heavier shoes.

An odd medical note—those foreigners who played host to mujalis managed to ward off the intestinal amoeba that attacked two of our teammates. At the end of three months in camp, all six of the foreign volunteers who had suffered mujalis emerged unscathed by amoeba in the bowel, while the two U.S. volunteers who had problems with amoeba-caused diarrhea never played host to mujalis. Amoeba are a serious problem; mujalis are not.

Mujalis bit our funny bones. The first ones located in camp had pounced on Olga's and Vladik's feet. It happened that the Soviets went off to Balcha during the Ephiphany holiday just after finding these mujalis. Since Ruslan cared for any medical problems we had and he didn't want to deal with these odd fellows, the trip to Balcha gave him a chance to turn them over to the doctors at Balcha. Ruslan announced as the Soviets left that he would have a surgeon at Balcha cut their mujalis out.

The Ethiopians thought that idea was hilarious. So many adult Ethiopians are accustomed to taking a needle and carefully scraping mujalis and their egg sacks out of a human foot, that the idea that a surgeon and a knife might be necessary for that simple operation seemed preposterous.

I discovered that the growth at the edge of my middle toenail was indeed a mujali on the very weekend in mid-February when the whole of the foreign team was staying at Balcha. Olga and Vladik had each had a second pesky set removed that weekend, and I had my first removed by a Soviet surgeon. I became doubtful about this method of treatment when, in the aftermath of the surgeon's knife, I felt more pain than the mujali had given me, and the bandage he applied was bulky enough to make me hobble.

Proof for my doubts came the week afterward, when I happened to see a spot on Jack's foot while he lay barefoot on our bed in the tent. He had never felt it. When it turned out to be a mujali, he requested quietly that Asellefech come and "operate." Without fuss, she came at midday and scraped out the egg sack with a needle. We sterilized the hole with alcohol, put a band-aid on it, and allowed it to do the only thing we expected it to do—heal.

In the end, our treatment changed altogether when Ruslan himself played host to a mujali. Since he didn't anticipate being at Balcha in the near future, Ruslan asked Gitachew to officiate. We all watched the operation one afternoon by the wash house. Our Soviet doctor sat on a rickety chair while Gitachew knelt, busy, in front of him. Ruslan was being rid of his pest by an Ethiopian expert. Snickers ceased. The faranjis had aculturated, at least with regard to mujalis. (Of the foreigners, only Sergei entertained no invaders. He appeared to have such a tough inner and outer hide that the bugs that attacked the rest of us gave up on him.)

Other medical matters were more serious. Early in our stay, Noel developed diarrhea, some nausea, and a fever that waxed and waned. When his symptoms persisted, Ruslan took him to Balcha for tests, and they kept him there. When we arrived at Balcha in mid February, Noel had already been in the hospital for a week to have his problem with amoeba treated. His blond, good-looking woman physician visited him for chats so frequently that, if he hadn't been feeling so rotten, he might have suspected her of conniving to keep him around. He didn't think he needed the IV's she insisted on to build his body up. Her conduct was always professional, however, and Balcha was a bleak place. Noel was happy for the chats, and the doctor must have relished having an intriguing stranger to speak with in Russian. After we'd brought him his violin, he had the added pleasure of playing Bach for himself and the lovely doctor.

Following some suspicious symptoms, Ann and I were also tested for amoebas during that weekend visit to Balcha. The results came back negative. Periodically, however, Ann continued to have bouts of diarrhea and vomiting. When she too spiked a more persistent fever, Ruslan wanted her to go back to Balcha for more tests. However, because Abebe waited in long gas lines that yielded only partial tanks or sometimes no gas at all, during the last six weeks of camp he brought the van from Addis only once a week with supplies. What was to be done to get Ann to Balcha? Besides, she was well into both the village work and teaching, and didn't want to miss teaching her English class for mere tests at Balcha. On a late weekend when Ruslan had persuaded Ann to return in the van with Abebe for tests, her illness came and went so erratically that, in spite of Ruslan's advice, on Monday morning when Abebe drove off, Ann decided not to go. Instead, she planned to take the International Center for Africa (ILCA) bus on Wednesday after one of her last English classes on Tuesday. The director of ILCA, an Irishman named Chamis, had been consistently helpful to our project. Whenever we arrived at the research center needing a telephone to call Roba in Addis or the U.S. (collect), he welcomed us in his own sparely furnished living room. Like us, ILCA employees suffered from the gas shortage, and so Chamis had also invited us to use the small bus they operated to Addis. It left the ILCA station each working morning and returned late each afternoon.

That Monday morning Ann and Senbet went off as usual to Gowa to work with the farmers. But by the time Asellefech and I returned for the noon meal, we met Ruslan, Noel, and Senbet roaring from camp across Godino. They said they were going to hire a horsecart and reach ILCA, ten kilometers off, fast! Ann had become ill again while working in Gowa, and Senbet had had to support her walking home. Now she needed to be "rushed" to the hospital, and the camp had no car. At ILCA Ruslan would plead for some additional vehicle Chamis could release to take Ann to Addis for this emergency, in spite of the gas shortage. Noel and Senbet were not only concerned, but they were both needed for translation.

Asellefech and I heard the news and hurried home to comfort Ann. The hot sun on her walk to Gowa had left her faint. Now she lay burning with fever in the tent she shared with Olga and Asellefech.

An hour later, as we were finishing lunch, a horn sounded at the gate. The guard opened it, and the driver of an ILCA van drove into camp carrying Ruslan, Senbet, and Noel. The makeshift ambulance bumped to a stop off the road and immediately in front of Ann's tent. Her suitcase was already packed. One more journey to the latrine, and the invalid was carted off with Ruslan.

At Balcha, Ann's first two days of treatment were rough. But five days later, when Abebe returned with the van and supplies, a pale young woman came with him. She had per-suaded the blond Soviet doctor to release her earlier than cautious medical judgment might recommend. The terms of her release included the return to camp with a raft of pills.

139

11.
Mood Swings: What! No Work?

I T WAS the subtler, work-related frustrations in camp that more seriously affected team morale. Early on, in mid-January, Roba and Belay had split us into three teams. Gitachew, Jack, Sergei, and Olga were assigned to construction, with jobs listed as mud-brick tukel construction, storage construction, road construction, and other construction.

Beriso, Vladik, Ruslan, and Noel were assigned to the farmwork, which included more double digs, compost pile construction, care of the fish ponds (they were finally sealed and stocked with fingerling talapia), and all other farm activities. Farmwork was always shared, however, with the food-for-work workers, who did the day-to-day work in the demonstration garden.

Asellefech, Ann, Senbet, and I were assigned to outreach work in Gowa and Godino; our work was listed as "school-based extension, contact farmers extension, women's involvment and participation in development, and house-to-house visits." We were asked to reach at least fifty contact farmers.

On paper the assignments of the construction and farm teams seemed possible, but in fact the work of these two teams was difficult to make happen. After we finished the two long double digs in the demonstration field, it was not clear what the next farmwork should be. The fish needed nurturing, and compost needed to be watered, but since Beriso had some forty food-for-work workers, farmwork seemed less essential to the foreigners. It took imagination and initiative to think of work to keep the faranji farm team busy.

Ruslan wanted to practice medicine and could do it more or less on his own with the help of translators. But he needed medicines and bandages, and our supplies were nearly exhausted. Vladik wasn't the type to be creative about making work initiatives. Noel, when he was not ill, looked after the fish but he had no equipment for thorough experimental work, and the fish seemed to take care of themselves. The farm team, then, had a tough time keeping itself busy.

The construction team was no different. Initially, Jack was pleased to have been assigned to the construction team, because that work fit the skills he had to offer. When the materials had not yet arrived for tukel construction, he saw his first job as building shelves the cooks had asked for in the kitchen. He measured, figured frugally, and asked Gitachew to purchase the materials he needed. Gitachew pulled out a stubby pencil to note the request and promised that when he was in Debra Zeit or Addis he would get the needed wood and nails.

Jack had noticed the first time he sat on one of our camp's chairs that it wobbled dangerously. Wooden chairs need regular maintenace if they're going to hang together. But wood to make furniture is scarce and expensive. No wonder Ethiopian village homes use wicker chairs, if they have chairs at all. All this meant that while he waited for shelving materials, Jack carved some dozen sturdy sticks and attached them to our camp chairs as braces.

When all the chairs were braced, Gitachew had still not purchased the wood and nails for the kitchen shelves. Jack asked him about it again. He made excuses. "I was too busy," "I didn't have the money," "I'll do it next week." Jack concluded that promises meant nothing.

Sergei, Vladik, and Olga had very little to do, and grumbled. Sergei assumed the role of the camp's "chronic complainer," and all of us became more unhappy than we might have been had Sergei not been so steadily critical.

While waiting for other work to appear, the construction team decided to dismantle the tukel that the Soviets on the first team had built. Belay, when he was in camp, had made pointed comments about its poor construction. When he'd been gone nearly four weeks working in the office in Addis, the team needed something to do, so they fashioned a new construction plan: tear down the Soviet-built tukel and prepare the same site to rebuild a model demonstration tukel, using the new mold to make better bricks that interlocked. Destructive work is dissatisfying. Sergei goofed off, and his example influenced Olga and Vladik.

Tensions rose and we called for a team meeting. Leaderless and with no materials for construction and no clear direction, we were floundering. If Belay was away, we still had to work out what we should be doing without him.

That evening, instead of leaving the dinner table we sat by candlelight determined to brainstorm ways out of our quandary. Noel had been thinking about the work so long and hard that he had written a critical letter to Roba. He asked to read it to us.

"The compost is drying out as it sits in the sun . . . the fish are doing all right, but we aren't involved enough in the experiments to measure the effect of fish-fertilized water on the crops." His tone was gentle, but complaining. "We ought to be teaching every village farmer with whom we work how to make a compost pile and why he should make compost to use on his crops." I watched the group as he read and saw that somehow the Ethiopians resented his criticisms and had stopped listening before he got to his positive suggestions.

Jack added forcefully, "We need a definite decision about how we should expand the camp facilities. We hear one day

Roba wants a storage building and the next day we hear he doesn't. Belay, who is supposed to tell us what Roba has decided, is always in Addis."

"We can't afford all those construction supplies." Gitachew bleated. Even by the dim candlelight I could see his frown.

"None of this work is important . . . " Sergei declared emphatically, and we hardly needed to hear Ann's translation to know he was griping.

Gitachew continued to waffle at all our suggestions for construction. "We . . . we can't afford that," he kept saying.

Finally, Beriso cut in decisively. "You are all wondering what to do because you haven't asked me," he said. "We need to dig another water storage pond to make watering the compost easier. The molds have come. We need to make mud bricks and build a well-constructed tukel for demonstration."

With only these two definite suggestions, the mood at the table picked up. As I sat in the near-dark, I found myself wishing we had held such a meeting earlier. If now we were acknowledging Beriso as our de facto leader, we might be able to have a sense of movement again. He might help us move out of the stalemate of our "in-camp" work. By candlelight, the team collectively switched gears and made decisions. To involve the Soviets we planned a new project: to dig another watering pond in the demonstration field. A second water depot near the compost would mean we could more easily maintain the necessary moisture in those piles, which at the moment were drying out fast in the hot sun. We decided the outreach team would return to all the contact farmers and make sure they knew about and made compost piles.

The next day it was clear that a heavy digging job appealed to Vladik and Ruslan on the farmwork team. Noel, in spite of the havoc the amoeba had wreaked on his system, did his best. There was still no wood for kitchen shelves, so Jack took to digging; but the hot sun and his age combined to leave him limp after only a few hours of heavy shoveling.

Olga and Sergei came to work each morning late. Sergei dug a little, Olga carried a bit of dirt, and then they stopped to snap pictures. They photographed the project's oxen plowing; they photographed the food-for-work workers sifting compost through a hand-made sifter; and they photographed each other in various calculated poses. Frequently, they disappeared from the work site early. The major effect of their work was to leave those working with them disgruntled.

After several days of exhausting digging, Jack decided Gitachew was never going to purchase the supplies he'd asked for, and so began to straighten nails and patch makeshift boards. With ingenuity, he fashioned several tiers of shelves in the kitchen, and the cooks were delighted with what he was able to create. Food supplies could be raised off the floor and onto shelves.

The shelves finished, Beriso recognized that Jack was capable of taking intiative in construction work and requested another building project of him. Jufari, the cook who made the injeera for our Ethiopian meals, had been using the big windowless tukel where the cooking oil used for payments to the food-for-work workers was stored. Beriso was, however, rightly nervous about building fires near this oil. He suggested that Jack use the mud bricks that had been salvaged from the de-constructed tukel to build a small house where Jufari could build her fire safely. That project fixed Jack's location behind the kitchen building and meant he could act as informal overseer to the food-for-work men making the new mud bricks.

The molds for interlocking bricks had come at last, and a mud pond was dug. Each day several young men hauled mud from the pond to a level spot near the kitchen, and crammed the mud into two molds. Once the wooden frame had been filled, it was removed and the wet mud brick left was allowed to dry. Many bricks were needed to build the new demonstration tukel. In camp, then, for that brief period Jack felt satisfied with his work. When the pond was completed, Ruslan busied himself with informal medical clinics and inventories of our dwindling drug supplies. But the other Soviets became increasingly more frustrated.

When enough interlocking mud bricks were dry and ready, it was decided to involve the younger Soviets in making the new demonstration tukel on the site of the one that had been torn down. Jack took over the supervision. A new, wider cement foundation was needed on which to place the mud bricks. Sergei seemed to enjoy the cement work, and lent it a sloppy enthusiasm.

Once, from a distance, I overheard Jack's irritated, raised voice, "Do you want to do a good job? Well, then, do it!" I guessed he was speaking to Sergei; his tone meant it didn't matter that Sergei understood no English.

But this building project, the first in several weeks the farm and construction teams were enthusiastic about, got diverted. Belay returned to camp with a different idea. Several rows of interlocking mud bricks were in place for the walls of the new tukel when Belay arrived. The food-for-work workers, he declared, should build the tukel because "they knew more about building such buildings." Belay may well have been right, but to take the work away from them devastated the foreigners' morale.

It began to be clear that the Ethiopian team members were also irritating each other. Gitachew tightly controlled the camp's finances. One day, as I lay in my tent in the midday heat, I heard Beriso's angry raised voice speaking in Amharic and the defensive tones of Gitachew. A few moments later when Beriso passed our tent, he stopped, still angry, to explain to me. His thin frame curled with exasperation as, quietly, he described the disagreement. Gitachew had refused to authorize a small expense in the nursery garden for an item Beriso considered essential. Another night I saw Asellefech speaking for a long time by candlelight with Gitachew, and when I asked her about it later, she would not tell me what the problem was, but it was clear she had in some way been hurt.

Further blows to the foreign team's morale came when the gas shortage made it apparent that we should suggest the cancellation of the first weekend trip out of camp. Our pride in ourselves for such "selfless" virtue hardly assuaged our disappointemnt at not seeing Soderi hot springs.

A month later, when we had hoped the gas shortage might ease, it was instead worse, and a weekend trip to Lake Langano, one of the Rift valley lakes, had to be canceled as well. Aside from one weekend in Addis, we had had no chance to leave camp, and the sameness had begun to wear on us. We needed a break, relaxation together.

One Sunday, when the Soviets had abandoned camp for the weekend, Belay realized that those of us left in camp had hit a "low" and needed a diversion. "Let's hire horsecarts and go see the three volcanic lakes of Debra Zeit," he proposed. All week my mood had been going up and down like a yo-yo. Whoop-te-do! A change of scene!

Noel was "under the weather" (we had to explain that idiom to the Ethiopians) and didn't go. Senbet, Jack, Gitachew, Ann, Belay, and I walked to the center of Godino where, by coaxing one of the drivers out of his house—it was Sunday and young men had to be dragged to work—we managed to hire three horsecarts.

Horsecarts are the transportation of those rural Ethiopians who are too ill, too tired, or too wealthy to walk. They consist of a single-axle, open, rubber-tired cart. Passengers perch on a wooden bench and place their feet in a well from which the shafts for harnessing the horse thrust forward. The bench is barely padded and just wide enough for two persons and a driver. Along the back edge of the bench runs an unpadded iron rail to prevent a passenger from sliding off the back. An unwary passenger may well leave the cart with a raw spot on the lower back from rubbing against that rail. Just as obese Ethiopians are rare, so are ample horses in Ethiopia. Sickly, bare-ribbed horses often pull these carts.

So, on Sunday three carts paraded out of the town square in caravan, one faranji and two Ethiopians bouncing on the seat of each cart. Gitachew and I were squeezed onto one seat together with our driver who, proud of the pace of his small brown horse with a blond mane, insisted on brandishing his whip and taking the lead. Each time the whip cracked, the little horse moved not one jot faster. I opened my bright blue umbrella to protect the three of us from the midday sun, and the driver flashed me a quick approving grin. The cart clattered over the dusty road, and the lack of space on the bench prevented Gitachew and me from looking each other in the eye. This was my chance. I asked Gitachew about his background. "I heard that my real mother died when I was one-and-a-half," he began in a low bass monotone, "and my father died when I was four." The shock of that kind of news reported matter-of-factly froze my glance straight ahead. I sensed Gitachew didn't want to look at me, either, as he continued. "A friend of my father wanted to take care of me. His wife was from the same area. At first they had enough, but they didn't know how to use their money. They began to be poor, so we didn't have enough food. I think I was about ten or twelve years old when they kept me at home and forced me to do housework. They punished me for playing with my friends. I needed relatives . . . but I was alone in the world."

Just then Jack and Senbet's cart, its dapple-gray horse straining, broke the gloom of what I was hearing by rolling past us. The western rock music blaring from Senbet's portable radio seemed to mock us. Our driver instigated a race, determined to maintain the lead. While our cart was involved in the delicate maneuver of passing on that narrow, dusty road. Gitachew was too tense to speak, and I was too tense to listen. Once we edged past the other trotting horse and regained the lead, I said, "We hear a lot in the U.S. about African orphans. I've never had the chance to speak with one."

"I was only one; there are many," Gitachew said softly.

"School was my one chance to escape. I liked going there and I don't know why, because at first I did not like to learn. Then, when I reached seventh grade, the family I lived with pushed me out. There was no place to go except to sleep with the night guards at the school. Sleeping there was not bad, but I couldn't find food, and I had almost nothing to wear." I tried to imagine what such a life would be like. But that desperation was too far out of my range of experience.

"When the school closed for the three months of the rainy season, it was harder because I was alone. I had nothing but a dry place to sleep. The first three days I found no food. I tried to go to the forest to cut some wood to sell. I gathered a bundle and took it to market, but when I reached the place at the market where the wood was sold, I saw my bundle was much smaller than the others' bundles. No one would want mine. It was raining hard, so I put my wood down beside the others and took shelter on a veranda. When I came back, it was like a miracle. There was a lady standing beside my bundle of sticks. She said she'd pay me fifteen cents (100 cents equal 1 birr) for it! If I carried it to her house for her, she would give me a piece of bread.

"That was the beginning of better luck. The next day was Sunday, and a schoolmate of mine was sure he knew a family who would take me in. My pride made me stubborn. I didn't want to depend on anyone. At first I refused to go to any family. My friend persisted. At last, when I saw my friend was so worried about me, I went with him. It was a good family and during that long vacation I found shelter with a farmer." I heard Gitachew say "good family" and recognized how differently he used that phrase than I might. In an American context "good family" might mean well-born, pedigreed, and of steady wealth. Gitachew meant a family that did not exploit him.

"The next year was my eighth-grade year, and I knew I needed to study hard to pass my exams at the end of it. I asked the farmer if I could go back to school at night to study and he agreed, but his wife didn't. The man still had jobs for me to do. I was useful to him in keeping his clothes clean and running errands, so he wanted to keep me. Almost three weeks passed in that way. But finally the wife's resistance—she didn't want me to go to school to study each night—became intolerable. I decided I had to leave that family and go live at the school again.

"My night study paid off. I passed the national exams with a good score. Six others from my school did well, and we were sent to compete nationally in another exam for entrance into the Agricultural and Technical School in Jimma run by the Point 4 Program through Oklahoma State University." There, staring straight out at the barren Ethiopian landscape without seeing it, I began to feel that it wasn't just hard work that had been operating for Gitachew through his boyhood. It was his intelligence.

"I got accepted to the program, but Jimma was a long way away, and to get there took money. Some good people in the town collected some money for me, but it wasn't enough to get me both home to collect my transcripts and to pay for transport to Jimma. I started by walking 180 kilometers home to collect my transcripts." Again, with frozen glance, I made still another judgment: intelligence would have gotten Gitachew nowhere without determination.

"When I finally came to Jimma I had almost no money left. The orientation for the four-year course in grades nine through twelve was difficult for me. The other students seemed more privileged than I was. I was in a new world, and I didn't fit. I didn't know how to manage. I bought a pair of shorts for nine birr, (the official rate in 1991 made one birr worth about fifty cents) a shirt for five birr, sandals for five birr, and one sock for fifty cents. That clothing had to last me four years.

"Every afternoon I went for horticultural fieldwork. But the strain! I wasn't like the others; it made my nose begin to bleed.

They couldn't stop my nose bleeding. They took me to the hospital, but I wasn't able to leave for a month.

By the time I was well I was so far behind I knew I couldn't make up the work. I was forced out of the Institute.

"There was no place to go but home. Maybe I could continue my secondary education."

At that moment we passed the huge spreading tree on the way to Debra Zeit. I looked up, hoping to absorb its lovely, green image as an antidote to Gitachew's story. But Gitachew continued with the account of his many failures, and I began to wonder: he had determination, intelligence; but perhaps nothing could help him make it in this unsophisticated culture, where psychological factors, in spite of going unacknowledged, still operate in determining a young person's success.

Gitachew's heavy bass voice droned on, telling me more stories of his fight to survive. Always his tale amazed me by its detail, including the people who had helped him, and how many birr he made for what work. He still remembered!

For this man, I thought sadly, every acquisition had been such a struggle that he remembered for a lifetime exactly what each item had cost and how many birr he had made for each bit of work he did.

"After the tenth grade I dropped out of school. I had no money to continue. Then one day there was another miracle. A missionary lady found me and became interested in me. She even offered me a job where I could be near her. I became an elementary school teacher. It was the first settled job I had, and it brought a regular income. That lady was the first to teach me that God cared about me.

"I never thought I'd get married and have my own family. I knew nothing about marriage. I knew nothing about family life. But a friend told me there was a girl whose grandmother had watched me since my eighth-grade school struggle. 'Why don't you marry her?' my friend asked."

When I heard this new turn I found myself relieved that someone thought Gitachew was an attractive marriage partner. His wife's grandmother must have figured his powerful build meant he was healthy, and health in itself makes a good marriage prospect in Ethiopia.

As I listened and bounced on that hard bench, Gitachew's voice lost some of its droning quality as he talked about getting married. "I told my friend he should not say another word. It was such a new idea for me, I felt I had to pray a long time about it. I wanted to continue my education, but my friend kept telling me it would be better if I married. I prayed. 'You're the one, Lord, who is looking after me, is it Your will?' After fifteen days, what seemed like a miraculous answer came to me: 'Take the girl.' We married when she was in grade five. My salary was 40 birr a month, 38.25 birr net. After the first year, a son was born to us. Fortunately they increased my salary that year by 15 birr a month."

Our caravan was nearing the outskirts of Debra Zeit. The people and donkeys and other horsecarts in the road were distracting me, but Gitachew was now recounting a better period in his life, and I needed to hear a more upbeat tale. While he and his wife had three sons and two daughters, he taught school at several places around Ethiopia. In one elementary school he rose to become director.

"Then my big chance came. The Ethiopian Evangelical Church asked me to teach in a new school for the deaf. They sent me to Gallaudet University in Washington, D.C., to study sign language and the psychology of the deaf. Afterward I worked in Addis teaching the deaf for five years until I grew restless and left there."

I asked why he had left a secure job just because he was restless. "I'm always on the lookout to better myself," he answered, "and now I also have to help my children to better their careers. Four of my children have finished secondary education, but they can't find work. They have succeeded in several entrance examinations, but so far it has all come to nothing. They sit at home without work."

There in Ethiopia I thought of Thoreau's phrase describing humankind as living "lives of quiet desperation," and I knew I was seeing yet another illustration. Thank God, I thought, that missionary lady had helped this man find some scrap of faith. I guessed she might have given him his first taste of thoughts that were not of desperation! "Sometimes," he said, "when I'm working with people—sometimes even when I'm at home with my family—I feel a loneliness. I am separated from everyone . . . everyone. That's when it seems only God understands me. God is all that keeps me from complete loneliness."

Gitachew was finished, but I found nothing to say. We fell into silence. My friend had exhausted his story, and for now I would solicit no more.

The carts reached the bottom of the driveway that led up to the Hotel Ras Hora. We climbed out of the horsecarts and Belay paid the drivers. They disappointed him, however, by refusing to agree to return for us that evening. By that time I didn't care that we might have to walk home; I was grateful to be on solid ground again. The six of us trooped into the hotel and onto the terrace overlooking the first volcanic lake.

We were disappointed to learn that the Ambo (a brand of mineral water) we had been able to order here during our first stay was unavailable now. The choices were Pepsi or beer. The Ethiopians and I ordered Pepsi; Jack, a beer. Ann drank nothing. She liked neither Pepsi nor beer, and ordinary water could not be trusted. Sitting on the hotel terrace, we gazed out through the trees at the blue-green lake, anticipating that later, when we were desperately hot from walking about town, we would return and swim. The priest at the Jesuit center had invited us to the center's beach on the lake any time we could get there. Today would be the first time.

That afternoon we trooped from one end of Debra Zeit to the other, riding in horsecarts when we could find them and walking when we couldn't. When we left in the late afternoon, we had seen all three of the deep lakes in the Debra Zeit area, and at the Jesuit center we had bathed in one of them.

The highlight of our discoveries, however, was the Debra

Zeit juice bar. On the highway from Addis into town, where those few cars privileged enough to have gas could conveniently stop, was a garden restaurant. We arrived there with the one o'clock crowd and found a rickety round table under a tree near a small, rough cement pool. We knew we were hungry. We had a choice of guava, avocado, orange, or papaya juice, or a mixture of these, together with popcorn. We asked for a menu and learned we could get Ethiopian hamburgers; but because they were expensive and of unknown quality, we ordered three for the six of us. The meat was a gristled, tough, small ball. Red pepper dominated its flavor. The bun was a coarse bread as nearly white as I had seen in Ethiopia. Catsup was the only condiment available. No wonder the main feature of this bar was juice!

The guava juice was thick, particularly flavorful, and refreshing. We all liked the papaya as it went the rounds. Even the avocado juice was interesting. We each sampled more than one kind, ordering at least twice and passing glasses all around our circle. Ann, who ate little meat, was happy to fill up on fruit juice. Jack paid for it all because it was his birthday.

At the Jesuit center, the lake was ice-cold. We edged our way in and came out refreshed. Then reluctantly we took ourselves back to the road to lean against the wall of the compound for half an hour in the lowering sun. No horse-cart that passed was willing to go to Godino; it was too late in the afternoon. Drivers could not expect to be hired for a fare on the return trip, and they didn't want to come back in the dark. Fortunately, at the Jesuit center we had met a French Canadian health worker on a rest weekend, and she had offered to drive us back if we could not find carts.

At length we accepted our defeat, returned to the center, took up her offer, and squeezed into her jeep. On the road we picked up Ann and Belay, who had thought they wanted to walk. Overcome by thirst, they were happy to ride.

It was intriguing to talk to another rural health worker in Ethiopia. She told us the gas shortage had only started to affect her village project in the north. She had heard about our project and wanted to see it. Once we reached camp, however, she took a quick turn through our garden, accepted a glass of boiled water, and drove off. It was not wise to be driving after dark, and that night she had sixty kilometers to cover to reach Addis.

I was back in camp with a nose that looked like it had been fried, hair arranged in dust clots, and a refurbished mood. That night I lay in bed thinking about the day. I remembered that when Jack and I were leaving for five years in Turkey, an American doctor who had worked there for forty years wrote to us with his good wishes. At the end of his letter, he added, "I rather hope you have some tough times; otherwise, how will you grow?" During our five years in Turkey I became aware of how wise that man had been to suggest we should expect trouble. Living abroad exacerbates problems and frustrations. But in retrospect the odd setbacks and unexpected troubles have somehow made our days abroad more memorable. That night, remembering those five years in the "sticks" of Turkey, the frustrations of this three-month period in Ethiopia seemed trivial.

And Gitachew's lifetime in this country? When, if ever, had it not been tough? Setbacks that last only three months don't have time to pervade one's whole experience and become obsessions. Besides, we were working with people who had endured—not triumphed, but endured —through whole lives that contained little more than a series of setbacks.

12.
Expectations: Holidays and People Will Change Them

ORKING closely with another person, anticipating having to accommodate to him or her, accepting another's working methods, can be a set-up for trouble. Not so with Asellefech and me. In spite of the differences between the cultures we come from, we found working together easy. The best times were not when we worked, but when we talked while walking the paths of Godino. Our chats were a ready window for each of us to the other's culture. We talked about the position of men and women in our countries, cultural attitudes, and sexual mores—anything that occurred to either of us was fair game. As we followed a village path we were at ease enough to exchange suggestions about each other's work styles. I learned that although Asellefech might be a tiny woman, timid in the face of dogs, she had skill as a teacher in both English and Amharic, tireless energy, and a giant heart in her slim torso. She learned that although I might be a pushy American, I had a good memory and useful organizational and follow-up ideas for our work with farmers. I needed her; she wanted me.

I discovered how essential Asellefech was to my feeling of belonging to the village on the next holiday, St. Mary's Day. The unique activity of this celebration, we heard, was that everyone in Godino visited each other's homes. Before the home visits, however, the faithful would gather at the schoolhouse around noon for a ceremony that would culminate in a procession to the Coptic church.

St. Mary's Day was more exclusively a Coptic holiday than was Christmas or Ephiphany. Asellefech was an Evangelical Protestant, not a Copt; and since St. Mary's fell in mid-week, she planned to stay in camp and observe it with me. That morning, in a holiday mood, we decided to deliver the nasturtium and sweet-pea seeds we had promised to Sisay and Dinberie, who had a spot where they wanted to grow flowers. We could stop there on the way to the gathering at the school.

When we arrived at Sisay's, he was bent over washing his head in the muddy irrigation ditch that ran beside their house. With water glistening in small drops in his black kinky hair, he looked brighter, still more handsome than ever. He wasn't embarassed to be caught at his morning ablutions; rather he studied the pictures on the seed-packets and seemed delighted to show us where he would plant nasturtiums and sweetpeas. Hearing our voices, Dinberie emerged from the house, and together they invited us to come back that afternoon after the celebration at the church.

The village had a different atmosphere that late morning. Everyone was moving in the same direction toward the school on the wide path. Some squatted just off the path selling wax tapers from piles on the ground beside them. Still others had a single religious picture to sell. The paths were lined with many more beggars than I had ever seen in Godino. Asellefech explained that the poor expected worshippers to be more open and giving on this day, since it was the day of the Mother of God, and Mary was known for her compassion.

When we reached the school courtyard a large crowd had already gathered and was listening to a priest's voice as it droned on. A group of bachelor-age men were singing and dancing off by the school garden patch, and after Asellefech had discovered she was not particularly interested in what the priest had to say, we wandered to the livelier spot. The young men had come all the way from Debra Zeit, rumour had it, and they sang in a brassy, rousing chorus as if they had two purposes: to attract attention and to practice for a later performance.

Restless, we returned to the main courtyard and strained to see over the gathered crowd. Several priests, dressed in their finery, stood passively under decorated umbrellas while other priests with staffs danced around them to the beat of a drum. After some ten minutes of chanting by the dancing priests and high-pitched keening by the crowd in praise (they believe St. Mary has brought all good into their lives) a procession started toward the church. As at Epiphany, the processing priests walked a distance, then stopped several times to allow other priests to dance in front of them.

Suddenly the procession changed character. The young men whom I had seen practicing launched out in front. Bold, chests high, like male birds puffing out their bright feathers to attract a mate, they trotted down the road brandishing sticks and singing. At one point a brash young drummer passed me and offered his drum for me to beat. I turned shy and demurred.

When the procession reached the church, the young bachelors trotted exuberantly into the courtyard ahead of the priests; the crowd came last. Once in the courtyard, the faithful milled about burning candles and greeting each other. Blank gunshots and high warbling wails pierced the air. People seemed friendlier to each other than they had at Ephiphany. A handsome woman greeted Asellefech and me. I thought I recognized her from a welcoming visit she had made to camp one day with her daughter, and I admired her national dress, which had particularly lovely embroidery on the edge of the shawl. She responded by inviting us to come to her home that afternoon.

Milling about the church courtyard, we bumped into Sergei, Vladik, and Olga. Ruslan, being a Muslim, was less interested in this day's Christian ceremony. Earlier that week I thought I had observed the younger Soviets making a more concerted effort to relate to villagers; on Tuesday they had gone to Godino market to take pictures. It didn't take long, however, to grow tired of gaiety punctuated by gunshots, and all of us soon headed home for lunch. Anyway, Asellefech assured me, the crowd would soon disperse to their homes for drinking and visiting.

That afternoon when we returned to Sisay's and Dinberie's home, holiday finery ruled. Dinberie's new dress was of teal-blue satin, and Sisay wore a gray sport jacket and gray pants. Mekdes had on a child's sweat-suit. She was fascinated by my blue umbrella and circled about pouncing on it just as an adored child in a North American family might tease for attention.

Refreshments were in order. First Dinberie passed chunks of bread in a bright basket. Then she brought us glasses of milk, which she said had been fermenting for several days. I realized there had been some kind of change in me, for I was so hungry for dairy products that I didn't give a second thought this time to whether the milk had been boiled or not. Sisay and Mekdes joined us in eating the bread, but Sisay would not drink the milk, since he said he and Dinberie were fasting and would abstain from any milk products for two months, until Easter.

When our glasses were nearly empty, three older women came in wearing the white cotton national dress. Dinberie introduced her mother from Debra Zeit. The other two women were the mother and sister of Dinberie's first husband, who had been killed in the war. While we sat chatting in the wicker chairs, bread was offered them—they also abstained from milk products. The women took our presence casually; a foreigner didn't put them off, I thought, as Asellefech translated for me unobtrusively. They spoke of things they might have mentioned had we not been present. They wondered how a woman they knew could have been seen begging at the St. Mary's Day ceremony. She used to be well off! Why was she now begging? She was still young enough to work!

After leaving Sisay and Dinberie's, we met on the path the woman whose dress I had admired at the earlier ceremony. With her son, she was on her way to a meeting, but when she heard we were headed for her house she turned back to come with us. It would not have mattered had we arrived and found her missing, for many other guests, both men and women, sat leaning against the walls of her main room. Their noise had the high pitch and jagged tempo that suggested the guests were drinking tala.

There were several dwelling units in this compound. Our hostess explained to us, as if she measured wealth in children, that she had twelve children, as she ushered us through the main house and out the back to a separate tukel.

Was it because she did not consider it appropriate to serve tala to Asellefech and me? At any rate, the tukel was new and lovely. It had a dried-mud bench all around its circular interior, and the mud walls here were uniquely decorated. The decorator had dipped a hand into orange paint and imprinted that hand countless times on the walls. The entire wall looked like a nursery school child's finger painting. Our hostess seated us on the circular bench and we were expected to join the ongoing conversation of the eight other guests.

One of the daughters of the family, dressed in a straight skirt and satin blouse and wearing no head scarf, seemed to be the hostess in this tukel, and she brought us a cool, watery drink and more bread. Then, as if she wanted to entertain her other guests with something that would include us, she told a story about a male mechanic who had worked on our camp's huge Soviet truck several months back. It seemed he had arrived in Godino with a young girl from Debra Zeit whom he had kidnapped. Somehow, he had wheedled an invitation to stay with this family, and they had given him a place to live with his young captive. No money was mentioned. The girl lay around the family compound all day for about a week while the mechanic discovered the truck was unfixable. At night when he returned to this compound, he acted as if he owned the home, and at length he made such a nuisance of himself that they had asked him to leave. He borrowed some money and left. Did we know what had happened to him and his captive? Asellefech remembered seeing a man working on one of our trucks, but she did not know. Wherever he might be, the daughter claimed, both amused and indignant, her family was better off rid of the amorous leech!

When we were ready to leave, the mother left with us, explaining that she and her son had been on their way to an important meeting. Godino had a cooperative to gather money for funerals, in particular for the tent and chairs that were standard funeral equipment. Her son told us proudly that he was the secretary of this cooperative. He carried a notebook under his arm to record the coop's proceedings and the money donated. Members earned money for the organization by making and selling food for bereaved families to serve to their fellow mourners. With those funds the cooperative was able to offer the tent and chairs free of charge. Clearly the woman took pride in being a member of one of Godino's going cooperative organizations, and she was pleased to be attending the meeting with her son. Her family, she indicated, was a pillar of Godino society.

On the way home, just before we reached the stream, four drunken young men hooted at Asellefech and me. In shaky English, they wanted to know about me: "Is she Christian?"

My answer, "Yes, I'm Christian," evoked hollered laughter and a joyful ruckus.

"It's tala that makes them Christian," I said. Asellefech slapped her arms across her stomach, curled up, and cackled.

Much earlier I had proposed that Asellefech help me arrange a series of interviews with village women. But from the time when Dinberie had walked to her home with us and I had my chance to question her, I saw that any note of formality in asking villagers questions might backfire. Village women had stories to tell, but I wasn't going to get them by sitting them down and asking for them. To work with the women was the way to know them and learn their stories.

Asellefech had indicated her hesitation about formal interviews by suggesting that certain questions would not be appropriate. She asked me to write out a list. I scribbled things like "What was the happiest moment of your life?" "What was the worst?" and remained uneasy. Village women didn't appear to think that way.

But there came a morning when I decided we knew Kenani well enough to ask if she might have a story she would be willing to tell us. On the way to the village, however, Asellefech told me of another stop she had in mind before we went to Kenani's. She had recently met a frail older woman who lived alone in Godino. The woman claimed to covet a double dig to grow vegetables, but there was no one to dig it for her.

This was the kind of story that activated Asellefech's giant-size heart and scheming talents. She went to Beriso and told him a woman had promised to tend the vegetables lovingly once the seeds had been planted. Would he release two food-for-work men for a morning to do the double dig for this woman? Beriso's heart was big, too, and he agreed.

When we arrived two young men were already sitting on the ground near a scruffy, abandoned tukel waiting for us.

We measured and put guide strings in place. The plot was only ten yards from the village irrigation ditch, an advantage, but there was no source of manure to add to the soil while preparing the double dig. When Asellefech asked her about manure, the old woman said she thought maybe all the kitchen garbage thrown onto the plot when the tukel was in use had replenished the soil.

When the men were ready to begin the double dig and the woman was nowhere to be found, I became uneasy. If she were not interested enough to be here when it was dug, would she follow through and care for the garden? We hung about for a short while after the men started, to make sure there were no problems. Then, since Kenani was nearby, we went to visit her, planning to return to check on the work later.

As we walked to Kenani's plot, I felt nervous. Would we catch her at home long enough to sit and talk to her? Would this, the first formal interview, succeed? We found Kenani in front of her tukel picking over lentils. Her ragged pullover sweater had a reindeer pattern across its yoke that I recognized from fifties-style American ski sweaters. Now the sweater was unravelling at the neck and pulled out of shape. (Another day I saw her son, Getu, wearing the same sweater.) Kenani went with us to inspect her carrots, having slung a dirty white cotton shawl across her shoulders, and folded her arms across her midriff as if, even in the bright sun, she couldn't get warm that morning.

We reached the bed and Asellefech bent to push a finger under the teff-straw mulch. Kenani pushed aside the mulch in another spot, and I chose a third. Was there a tiny germinated fringe of green? When all three of us had found a germinated seed, Asellefech asked casually if Kenani would answer some questions I had. She nodded, and the three of us planted ourselves beside the carrot bed. Asellefech and Kenani sat on their haunches, and I sat flat in the dust. As she spoke, the dark image of Kenani's stately profile against the light embedded itself in my memory.

Asellefech began with business. Had Kenani spoken to any of her neighbors about doing double digs with us? "They're suspicious," Kenani said. "When the seeds you plant are harvested, they think you'll demand the crop."

Asellefech frowned, recognizing the same doubts yet again. Gently, she reassured Kenani: "A farmer's work to dig the double dig helps us further our work, so we furnish the seeds." Watching Kenani's face, I sensed she had expressed doubt as much for herself as for her neighbors. Something for nothing? When did that ever happen? Getu's work, however, could hardly be considered "nothing."

At last, prompted by another question from Asellefech, Kenani began to speak about her life, quietly, in a low voice. Her voice was dull compared to the animation of her ordinary tone. She took long pauses for translation as if she, too, wanted to consider each thing she told us.

First, she told us of her husband: "He was a good man and worked hard before he went blind. . . . He was always blind in one eye, and then something [I guessed it was a cataract] grew over his other eye." She sighed. "At times I'm tempted to leave him and go to Debra Zeit. I could work there for one of the Russian housewives and make good money. But I can't do that. He was a good man." Now as she spoke, she fingered her white shawl and her voice broke. "We are poor now, and I'm cold at night. Nothing keeps me warm at night but this shawl." With the hot morning sun beating on us, undramatically she hugged her breast and shivered.

Then her thoughts must have shifted to Gitachew, her son whom she called Getu. "I promised St. Mary I'd put a stone on my back and cross four rivers if only she would give me a son. But then when I got a son, he was no good. St. Mary let me down." She shook her head and paused to think of an illustration. "I'm always afraid he will turn into a thief." A while ago, near their garden plot, Getu had gathered wood and brush and begun to build a corral for a cow. He had built the corral half way when some boys came along and accused him of stealing their wood to make it. Kenani had stood up for her son. "The people of Godino must judge whether Getu has stolen your wood," she told his accusers. Instead of backing off, the boys began to stone Kenani's house and yard, and continued for several weeks. Relief came only when the village authorities accused the accusers themselves of being thieves and took them off to prison. Kenani was relieved on two counts. The stoning stopped, and if the boys who accused Getu of thieving were thieves, that seemed to indicate Getu was not. Kenani herself was still not certain.

Her daughter, who lived in Godino and quarreled with her husband, had married a man who was better off. We asked if she had won the battle with her husband about whether to sell the calf. Kenani shrugged. They were raising it.

After a gentle sigh, Kenani returned to speaking about her husband. "He does nothing now but sit outside all day and doze." Her voice broke again before she caught herself. "But really," she straightened her back as she squatted, and said earnestly, "I am a happy person." Remembering her usual liveliness and how often I'd heard her joking, I knew she meant what she said, and was glad when her neighbor, Dinkenish, arrived to ask us a question. Kenani just didn't enjoy talking about herself, and I didn't enjoy making her do so.

Dinkenish was younger, and by contrast with Kenani's bright eyes, hers were velvet-fawn eyes. A smudged pink dress hung slack over her thin body, and her collar bone protruded from its V-cut neckline. Kenani always wore a black scarf wrapped around her head so that its ends crossed in front. Dinkenish's scarf, of a gayer color, was pulled straight across her forehead and tied in back. When she smiled, I saw she had a protruding upper gum with only two front teeth. She moved straight to business. "I'd like to have a double dig," she said, "but my husband is sick and there is no one to dig it for us."

In English, Asellefech and I consulted. I spoke evenly as I expressed my doubts. Even though I used a language our friends didn't understand, I wanted to be sure my tone in no way conveyed a caution that Dinkenish might detect. I worried that she might have heard of the old woman for whom we were digging, and that if we arranged for the released time of any more food-for-work workers, we might be deluged with requests from other villagers. Ought we to foster that kind of dependency?

Asellefech was a diplomat. In Amharic, she told Dinkenish, "We have the seeds and would like to plant them with you, but you will have to do your own double dig." Dinkenish was perhaps fifteen years younger than Kenani and looked strong. She said she and her daughter would try.

Kenani went with us as we picked our way through the clumpy hills of dry grass to Dinkenish's garden patch, where we measured off a small plot for carrots. Walking back past Kenani's tukel afterward, I moved thoughtfully, still in the spell of the impressive dignity and balance I had sensed in this woman's tale of a difficult life. Then, saying goodbye, Kenani and I were moved to hug each other. In that embrace her vehement kisses didn't come in the ritualistic pattern of the three alternating cheeks according to Ethiopian custom. High feeling overcame both of us.

We passed by the old woman's plot again. Were the food-for-work men goofing off with no one to oversee them? We found them hard at work. That afternoon the woman's plot was ready, and we planted carrots the next day. Her crop, however, did not turn out to be impressive. She opened the irrigation ditch to water it inconsistently, and she was slow in removing its mulch.

Kenani had told us about another woman, Zeynash, who might like to do a double dig, and that late morning we headed for her two-room corrugated iron house on a prominent corner of the village. Zeynash was tall and stately, with light skin and large bones. She appeared to be only about forty, but her daughter, Abubavitch, held an eleven-month-old baby whose hacking cough made us uneasy. The mother and daughter proposed to dig two tiny plots just outside their house. We measured the beds, Asellefech explained how the double dig was done, and we all retreated inside for coffee.

Zeynash laid a goat skin for us to sit on a wide wooden bench against the back wall of the largest room of the house. This house, like so many others, had light only from its door, and in a dark corner I could just barely see eight burlap bags plump with grain, a prosperous sign.

As Zeynash prepared the coffee, she told us her husband had died suddenly some five years ago, leaving her with two older daughters and two smaller children. One of the small children, a sturdy barefooted girl, stood beside the grain sacks staring at us adoringly. Her second oldest daughter sat squatting, her hands flying to crochet a doily. Often we had seen women and young girls weaving baskets of sisal, but this was the first time I had seen anyone working with cotton thread. As she worked she told us she usually lived with a relative in Debra Zeit, where she attended the high school. She was at home now because it was vacation.

While we waited for coffee, Abubavitch's baby had a coughing attack. Its chest sounded alarmingly tight, and I asked if she had seen anyone for medical advice. She hadn't. "If you want to take him," I said, "there is a Soviet doctor in camp who would be happy to examine the child. He has no drugs, but he would give any advice he could." Abubavitch decided she would take the baby to camp, and before we left I wrote her a note of introduction to Ruslan, which of course he would have to have translated, since he knew no English. He told us later that he was happy to see the baby, but he was concerned the child might have chronically weak lungs.

Zeynash produced three small Chinese tea cups of coffee, complete with green grass on the serving tray, and a stick of incense burning near the door. While we drank the coffee, Abubavitch, who had handed her child to the youngest, tiny sister to hold, passed a basket piled high with chunks of bread from which we broke small pieces. The girl turned, then, and passed the basket to four children lolling near the piled grain sacks, watching us. Two of them stared with their fingers in their mouths, and Zeynash explained that they belonged to a neighbor. Rapidly, without the ceremony involved in making it, we drank the coffee. Then, although I wondered whether it was polite, we left immediately after emptying the small cups. In Turkey it would have been an insult to leave so soon after finishing coffee offered ceremonially. Asellefech claimed we could politely leave at any time. Ethiopia lacked protocol as to when it was acceptable to leave after finishing one's coffee. Walking back in the glaring noon sun, Asellefech and I talked about our progress. The word was going around. The potentially more self-reliant in Godino were beginning to seek us out. But for me there were only seven weeks left. Would we be rolling well by the end of my stay?

13.
All My Trials . . .
Won't Soon Be Over

ONCE we had acquired new contact farmers in Gowa, the outreach team split up. Each morning Ann and Senbet walked off to Gowa, and Asellefech and I to Godino.

Focusing only on Godino encouraged Asellefech and I to think of that village as "ours," and the families we worked with, their trials and successes, as special to us. One morning walking in Godino alone, I came to a place in the path where the irrigation ditch had to be forded with a healthy leap. At that moment I knew two things: which spot of level earth would brace my foot for a successful jump; and because I knew where to put my foot, I belonged in the village.

More importantly, we were becoming involved with the lives of the villagers. One event boosted that sense of involvement in Godino life. One morning when we arrived at her home, Kenani announced she couldn't keep her appointment with us to transplant beet seedlings into her garden because she had to take a friend to the clinic. The friend, a widow from another village, had bloody stools. The ailing woman had tried various remedies, including going to traditional healers in her own village, but nothing had helped. That morning she had appeared at her friend

Kenani's house in pain and asked for help in going to Negash's clinic.

Since Kenani couldn't work with us, we went instead to plant the carrots of a teenage boy, Zeynebe. In spite of a badly malformed foot, Zeynebe had eagerly dug a double dig, and was now ready to plant it.

The next day, we wondered how Kenani's friend was doing, and stopped to see her. Inside Kenani's dark tukel we could scarcely make out the patient, lying wasted and weak behind a partition. Her breath came in rasps and her low moans of pain were constant—I sensed that the woman was dying. I suggested to Kenani that I might get my physician husband to bring something to relieve her pain. Did she want a visit from a foreign doctor? Yes, she said.

Asellefech and I went straight back to camp to persuade Jack to leave his construction project. I thought he might be willing to bring some of the pain killers that were part of the stock of medical supplies he carried everywhere. Jack was always hesitant to preempt Ruslan's position as the camp doctor, but since the Soviet was away on some other medical mission, it was easier to convince Jack to come. He brought three pills with him.

When we arrived back at Kenani's, the woman still lay moaning behind the partition. Jack leaned over her and slowly, gently, did a cursory examination. She was shy when he palpated her abdomen, but his soothing voice, even in a language she could not understand, eased her. Her low moans ceased momentarily. After a few moments he stood straight again to speak to Kenani. "She is very ill," he said, and Asellefech translated. "Probably the only hope for her would be to get her to the hospital in Debra Zeit. But," he shook his head, "Even that might not be helpful now, when she is so wasted."

Tears came to Kenani's eyes. She nodded. Jack pulled three pain-killing pills from his pocket, gave them to Kenani, and twice repeated the instructions as to how she should administer them to help her friend's pain. Kenani listened, said she would give her one immediately, and we left. Nothing more could be done.

In the early afternoon we stopped by Kenani's tukel again. She wasn't home, but her blind husband and the dog sat companionably outside in the sun. The dog recognized us and didn't bark. The old man reported that their house-guest had stopped moaning and seemed more at peace. She was sleeping.

The following morning we heard the drums that signify a death in the village and learned that, at about five in the afternoon, the woman had died.

Dinkenish, the woman who had wanted our workers' help in digging her double dig, was Kenani's neighbor. In the end she had persuaded her husband, Tadese, to summon his small energies to do the digging. He had been ailing for nine years, but he managed to prepare a double-dig bed in which we planted carrots. The day we planted them he joined us, but when we left briefly to check on someone else, we returned to find him lying in pain, knees to his chest, in his field. The strain of the planting had been too much. "But the effort was worth it," he insisted, "I want carrots!" He said he had more space in a gulley on the other side of his tukel, and he would prepare beds there for cabbage and beets. We arranged to return to show him how to make a compost heap.

When we arrived the next day, Tadese was still exhausted, but he came out to where we would make the pile and perched on the ground, knees crooked, to hear what we had to say about compost's usefulness. "It makes sense to make use of materials at hand," he said, "because I have no money to buy fertilizer." Dinkenish was ready to work with us, and a seventh-grade boy, Alemayo, for whom we had arranged to plant carrots, happened to meet us that day at Dinkenish's house. Alemayo saw that Tadese was hurting and helped dig the shallow compost pit. All four of us gathered the green material and dung to layer the compost pile, and before we left we gave Dinkenish instructions. She should water it, add another layer, then keep adding and watering.

Having given Dinkenish a start, and pleased with Alemayo's volunteer help, we went to the lad's house to inspect the bed he had dug. When working with youngsters, we were more careful to see that the beds they prepared were actually twenty-four inches deep. His bed was deep enough, and so we planted.

There was a certain irony in Alemayo's digging the compost pit for Dinkenish's family. Dinkenish and Tadese had seven children: six daughters and a sixteen-year-old son. Dinkenish told us that they felt themselves to be too poor to feed their son. He lived with and worked for another family in the village, but was not happy there. Dinkenish and Tadese could have used the help of their own son, rather than that of Alemayo, but he'd been sent off because they thought they could not afford to keep him at home.

One afternoon, when we knew them better, we suggested that if Tadese wanted some medical advice, he would be welcome to go over to camp and speak with one of the doctors. He nodded, indicating he might do that, and that afternoon he showed up at a time when Jack was there alone and couldn't consult with Ruslan on the diagnosis. Jack readily identified that Tadese had a type of abdominal hernia that was dangerous only if it became strangulated. Whenever it got out of place, however, it was painful.

The next day when we saw Tadese, his mood had lightened: the nine-year mystery had been cleared up. He knew what was wrong! He told us that he'd decided to put his name on the government list to have the operation performed and financed. While he waited, he assured us, he was better off just to know what it was that ailed him. He proved he was feeling better by digging and planting three more small double-dig beds for cabbage and beets. We lent a watering can to the two families—Kenani's and Dinkenish's fields were close together—so that they could more easily water their tiny seedlings, and Tadese volunteered to be responsible for keeping track of the can's travels from family to family.

About this time, a group of twenty-five Ethiopian relief workers gathered for a conference in Debra Zeit. Since the purpose of the conference was to explore ways to better involve the village folk with whom they worked, they asked to come and observe our work. One woman conferee told me hers was a village project to promote prenatal and child healthcare. She feared, however, that when the project pulled out of the area, their efforts might be forgotten because of administrative top-heaviness and inability to involve the people with whom the project worked.

Another conferee who had been working in Eritrean relief told me that the drought and the war had vastly complicated relief work in that area. His project had found it impossible to consider developing indigenous education projects. He was attending the conference so that if the war ever ended, he would be prepared to help his relief organization begin to implement its dreams.

Accompanied by a small group of conferees, we walked to the village to introduce them to some of our contact farmers and see the double-dug garden patches. Kenani's dog, who had become accustomed to Asellefech and me, barked in a terrible rage at these new strangers. Kenani wasn't home, but both Dinberie and Tadese showed off their beds and chatted with the visitors.

The construction of a double dig sounded complicated to these conferees, and they asked to see one in the making. We took them down to a new contact, Ambasu, who we knew was in the middle of digging his bed. Although he himself was away, his pretty wife, Matakya, and their three small children were at home. Matakya always startled me when she opened her mouth to speak. Her voice had the high pitch and laconic expression of a child's voice. Her baby tones nearly made it impossible to think of her as the nursing mother she was. That day, with three children clinging to her skirts, she explained competently to the conferees how her husband was digging the double dig.

Walking back across the fields to camp, one of the conferees challenged me. "How can you be certain your work will have any lasting effect?"

"There's no way I can be certain. We're teaching useful methods in the village. That's all I know," I said. "The project hopes to help make the villagers' soil more productive and their yields more varied."

"But what will happen when you're no longer in the village?" Still friendly, our visitor continued to press me.

"Even when we're not here these methods are still feasible—all they require is human effort with hand tools. But," I admitted, "I won't know if they go on using these methods."

"Why, then, are you introducing them?" he asked.

"Because they are good methods and . . . I feel good about introducing them." Hesitantly, I defended myself.

Although I didn't quote it at the time, I remembered something Albert Schweitzer wrote: "No ray of sunshine is ever lost, but the green which it awakens into existence needs time to sprout, and it is not always granted for the sower to see the harvest. All work that is worth anything is done in faith."

Our work with Zeynebe, the lame lad, had more immediate results. At his house was a double dig that we had planted with him, and we returned several times to check it. His carrots sprouted well, and we had made a compost pile with him. While working with him I became curious about his leg and asked Jack what he thought the boy's problem was. Jack guessed that he might have had polio as a young child, since only one leg's growth had been stunted. He went barefoot, since no shoe would fit his misshapen foot, and walked bobbing up and down, with his weight shifting to the toes of his short leg.

One day while passing Zeynebe's compound, as was our habit, we stopped to see how his carrots were coming. Was he watering, and had he removed the mulch? Zeynebe was not at home, but his mother came to speak with us. Clearly, she was embittered about something. We concentrated on what had happened to Zeynebe. His carrot sprouts were neglected. Why, we wondered? He had been conscientious up to this point.

In a rush of angry words his mother began the story. The village headman had accused Zeynebe of stealing wooden poles from the store of wood that belonged to the village, and had thrown him in prison. With great difficulty the lad's father had paid a bribe and gotten his son released. Now Zeynebe was dispirited and determined to take revenge by letting his carrots die.

Wasn't that a useless way to take revenge? we asked. His mother agreed with us, but she, also, was so bitter she didn't know if she could persuade Zeynebe to begin to care for his garden again. "The village heads are down on us," she declared. "They took my first two sons for soldiers. Both of them were killed. Now we have only this one son left and he is lame, so they won't take him, but they still make our lives miserable. We will have to leave this village." She spoke harshly, but tears came to her eyes.

I noticed that her dress had holes that showed the nipples of her breasts, as if her breasts had leaked milk so often that the cloth had rotted and dropped out. Since Zeynebe was around thirteen, I guessed that dress had been worn a long time, unless she'd lost another younger child.

When she'd finished her tale, she asked us if there was a possibility Zeynebe could be hired as one of the food-for-work workers. He was a good worker, but the family's fields did not yield enough income. Asellefech and I left without making promises. We'd be back that afternoon, we said, to speak with Zeynebe about his carrots.

At the noon break we asked Beriso if there were any vacancies on the food-for-work roster. He had just had to let someone go and was not sure about hiring anyone else. We could tell Zeynebe, however, that in a week he could come and inquire.

At the family`s compound again, we banged on the gate. Zeynebe opened it, but as he stood before us his eyes remained lowered in his long face.

Asellefech spoke to him soothingly, but he remained subdued and refused to meet her eye. "Don't you want to eat carrots you've grown, no matter how badly you've been treated in the village?" she asked. The boy didn't answer. Only when we told him that in a week he could come over to camp and see Beriso about a food-for-work job did he raise his chin and offer a slight smile. We sensed as we left that he might water his carrots.

Zeynebe waited only three days. The following Monday Beriso told us he had turned up, asked for work, and been given it. Beriso also told us later that of all the food-for-work workers Zeynebe was the most conscientious, arriving early in the morning to take care of his assigned beds and working more steadily than others who had no bare, lame foot.

Some of our work was undertaken simply because we found a certain villager willing and lively, not because we expected the new methods to have a permanent effect. Wode Boru was one such woman.

Wode's one-eyed husband—he was never around long enough for us to learn his name—had taken us out to measure beds for double digs on our very first day in the village, but he had not dug them. We bumped into Wode frequently, and whenever we inquired whether the plot was ready, she shrugged. Her husband had not yet done it. Always she wanted to know if we would come to her tukel for coffee? No, we refused to come, insisting we would not drink coffee with Wode until the day we planted carrots with her in her double dig. Secretly, I very much hoped the ploy would work. Wode was a talkative woman, and I was curious about her stories. Coffee would be the time we might get them. But when we'd been working some five weeks in Godino, she still had no beds ready to plant.

Then one day Wode saw us walk past her compound carrying cabbage seedlings to transplant into another farmer's beds. She stopped us for a look, and her covetous nature sprang into action. Those cabbage seedlings were absolutely necessary to her in her own beds! "There is a girl living with me now," she told us. "She'll dig the double digs." When we next passed, Wode and a big-boned, dark-skinned thirteen-year-old girl, Almaz, waylaid us. Would we give Almaz instructions? Of course we would.

As if she owned the place, Almaz took us to the garden plot. We re-measured, gave her instructions, and went off promising to return two days later when she might have had time to dig the beds. Almaz and her younger brother had been "given" to Wode by their parents for food and shelter in return for work. Almaz cooked and gardened while her younger brother herded Wode's cows.

When we passed the compound the following morning, Almaz came out to tell us that she was ready to plant. We checked the beds and found that one was indeed ready and the other one was near. We promised to bring seeds that afternoon to plant, and Wode, who had nosed into the conversation, added with glee that she would prepare the coffee.

The carrots didn't take long to plant, and we were soon gathered around the outdoor fire where Wode, who had not deigned to get her hands dirty planting, was preparing coffee. Dinberie and Mekdes came across the path to share in the party, and Almaz brought goat-skins for Asellefech and me to sit on. The others took up squatting positions. Wode explained that usually they perform the coffee ceremony inside; but because it was St. Gabriel's Day, they were making it outside. One of her blackened clay coffee pots had belonged to her mother, and she was using it in her mother's memory.

Mekdes, as always, prattled eagerly and became a center of attention. Wode tried to teach her to take my white hand and bow her head in greeting. It was too much. She didn't bow, but she did return my smile, plunk down next to her mother, and begin to sing little ditties.

Dinberie told a story about a very black three-year-old in the village whose name meant "bride." They had nicknamed her "faranji," Dinberie said, because the child was so dark as to be different. Dinberie told also about seeing a black boy-child on a path in the village naked. Her first idea was that she might be seeing Satan. This light skinned woman's stories seemed to indicate that in the village dark skin color was somehow less desirable.

Wode was eager to tell us her story. Squatting, pounding her coffee in the wooden mortar with a wooden pestle, she explained to us that her present, one-eyed husband was her sixth. She had lived with her fifth husband thirty years. He was the one she truly loved, in spite of the fact that he was an old man. Her wealthy father had disapproved. "You shouldn't live with such an old man," he had insisted. She paid her father no heed, and to assert his command her father had taken his daughter by force to her brother's in Addis to keep her away from the old man.

"I had no appetite. I grew weak . . . sick. Finally after three months my husband came to ask about me. My brother told him I was crying all the time and didn't want to eat. So my husband took me back again to my home in Godino, and my father gave up.

"You see, I loved that husband because he gave me freedom. He knew when I left the compound to go out at night that I was going for sex to someone else, but he let me go. My first four husbands had all beat me when I left like that. I had beautiful eyes and teeth, and other men desired me."

Asellefech, hardly shocked at the story she was translating for me, was nonetheless curious about issues it raised. She asked me if in the West we had a word that described a woman of unusual sexual appetite. I told her we called such women nymphomaniacs. She said there was a word in Amharic, *kinseranya,* for such a woman, and after she named it she and Wode and Dinberie spoke of it frequently in the conversation which followed. I recognized it several times. Wode entered freely into this conversation about her own idiosyncracy.

Asellefech confirmed what I had sensed in Wode's manner. She seemed proud of her nature rather than shy or

177

ashamed of it. When Dinberie speculated that a woman with so many lovers must end up childless, as Wode had, all the women snickered.

Later in the conversation Wode told me she'd heard there were doctors at our camp. Had they tetracycline? I said, yes, there were doctors but they had no medicines. Wode wondered if in return for their services, the doctors might be interested in her favors. I didn't try to answer that. Instead, Asellefech asked Wode if her present husband beat her. "No, I'd kick him out if he did," she said. "It's my house, my wealth. I control it."

Wode's wealth was nowhere very evident. I could not recall ever seeing her dressed in anything other than a plain, dark green dress, which was usually grimy. She had one tiny ball of gold as an earring. Always her craggy face was topped by a plain black head scarf. Her eyes, however, had a faded luster that suggested they had once been as lovely as she claimed. Her gleeful pride, the sense of self she showed in the telling of her past, was unforgettable.

Almaz, who could only guess her age as thirteen when I asked her, had promise and intelligence of another kind. Steadily busy weaving baskets, making bread, getting sugar cane ready to take to market and sell, she never waited for a prod from Wode. She behaved as if the crops and belongings in the compound belonged to her as much as to Wode. More than once as we were leaving, she broke off pieces of sugarcane to give to us to suck on. Once when we arrived at Wode's, Almaz was away in the mountains. A headache had sent her to the mountains to find healing waters. In no way did her self-starting nature contain a sense of drudgery.

Walking home from that coffee session with Wode, Asellefech and I caught up on the translation of parts of Wode's story I had missed. I was also curious to pin down what Asellefech had learned about Almaz. Finally, we fell silent. In the silence the phrase of the old spiritual came to me, "All my trials, Lord, will soon be over." How far that sentiment was from the thinking of these people! I had begun to have some sense of the trials of these villagers, yes, and oddly it seemed to me that none of them could count on their trials being soon over. But they didn't seem to look toward death. Life asked of them endurance, and that's what they gave it.

These villagers didn't appear to know how poor they were, because they knew so little about the wealth of the rest of the world. They accepted a life of struggle because they had no idea what else was possible. They lived with their trials and seized upon celebrations to forget them. Some of them found meaning in hard work, others didn't. No one in the village was desperately hungry because they knew each other well enough to prevent that, but neither was anyone living on easy street, for there were no easy streets. Health and crop failures, death, thievery, and seizures for the war front were givens in this basic life. Their antidotes—birth, education, hard work, and humor—only worked at times. The simplicity of their lives could never lure me, but I admired it.

A certain sense of privilege was blossoming in me. When heading for Ethiopia I hadn't anticipated I would begin to feel so fond of persons of a background so different from mine. Nor could I anticipate the varied personalities with whom I'd rub shoulders. Almaz was a uniquely capable, illiterate thirteen-year-old. And Wode? She was of a type I'd had few chances to listen to, ever!

14.
Mud Balls, a Party,
and Rumors of War

ETHIOPIANS told us in March that the short rainy season was due, but what came was only its harbinger: dour clouds and a few drops each afternoon. Then one night it rained real water. We didn't know our tent leaked until I put one bare foot on the floor in the middle of the night to get up, and it sloshed into a film of water!

At no time did the differences in Jack's and my temperaments emerge as sharply as in our reaction to a wet tent. My laziness showed in a certain sanguine acceptance: I was for curling up, letting our sleeping bags go warm-soggy, and dozing as we could. Jack, on the other hand, fussed and fiddled. To curl up and endure without doing something to stop the flow of water into our tent was temperamentally impossible for him.

That first night Jack got up and did whatever he could to channel the flow of rain away from the tent's seams, where it appeared to be leaking. It was impossible to sleep. I lay in my bag cheering him on, justifying my lethargy by doubts that anything would help. Leaky roofs, I calculated, must be a given of the thatch on the older tukels of many of our village friends. If the villagers were resigned to water in their dwellings, we should try to accustom ourselves to leaks as well. After two hours the wind died, the rain stopped, and we slept.

In the morning Jack got up and began to fuss in earnest. When he was finished, a jaunty awning overhung the top of our tent and channeled the rain off the roof and into small trenches he had dug in the ground to lead the water away. Other teammates whose tents had leaked puttered about rigging other solutions. Beriso's tent was the oldest, and he decided to move from the large, ancient, rotting tent to the camp's one tukel, which until now had been used for storage, despite rumors that the dirt-floored dwelling had mujalis. Beriso must have figured that he'd rather have a bug invasion than a soggy bed.

Once Beriso's large tent had been vacated, Noel moved his smaller tent inside Beriso's old emptied one, calculating that two canvas covers might give him a better chance of staying dry. Ruslan watched all the makeshift preparations skeptically, dubbed Beriso's tukel Mujali Hotel, and scoffed. His attitude seemed more like mine. Villagers endure it, we can too! All those who had made adjustments, and even those who had not, waited in defiance for the next onslaught of rain.

It came three nights later. The second rain was relentless and came with a fierce wind. Bango! It tore Jack's awning loose to flap noisily on our tent. Still, in the morning we found the persistent rain had penetrated our tent much less heavily than the first night's short rain.

The second storm, however, had badly damaged the tent belonging to Olga, Asellefech, and Ann. The wind so tore at one end that the wet canvas had crashed down upon Ann's bed. Fortunately, she wasn't sleeping there that night. She was a patient at Balcha. When there was a collapse at the other end of her tent, Asellefech had risen without fuss and joined our cook, Edil, in her tent. Olga? She had scarcely roused.

When we woke the morning after, a dismal rain was still falling. Noel and Beriso huddled in the wash house rubbing their hands and comparing notes. Their separate ploys had kept them dry. Jack worked to restore our canopy. Since the rain prevented him from hanging his blankets out to dry, Ruslan busied himself somberly lacing the collapsed part of the women's tent. Would the remaining half survive the next wind? I stood with Olga and Asellefech, huddled in the wash house, feeling unable to do anything. In merely walking across camp to the latrine my boots had collected such gobs of gumbo, it felt as if I walked with two bowling balls clinging to my feet.

Watching Ruslan struggling stoically in the rain, I was moved. Here was the same man who, in the early days at Balcha, had found an outlet for his gallantry in peeling bananas to look like flowers. Now, when our needs were more basic, he was still finding gallant gestures. Senbet and all the other men eventually joined him.

I felt guilty merely looking on. Then I remembered that two weeks before, when Ruslan had returned to camp after sleeping a night out to watch for dik-dik (a small deer), I had helped him. Having slept in a haystack, Ruslan returned with his wool blanket smothered with small bits of hay that clung and would not shake off. After hanging his problem on the camp's community clothesline, with his stubby fingers he began to remove the hay one piece at a time. The task was endless. Observing his slow progress, I joined him in picking away at the pesky bits. Ruslan was clever at communicating good will without words. Just that once, I comforted myself, I'd found a small gesture to return his good will.

At around ten o'clock that morning the rain stopped. Finally Asellefech and I could go to work. But when we took our usual route to the village, we discovered the stream was too high to cross. The stones we usually used to jump across were a good foot under water. Downstream, at another spot where we sometimes crossed, the huge boulders were well washed with water, but there was one place, narrow and deep, where we could jump across with care.

The stream raged beneath us, and on the far side the rocks

rose high above the path. We had to sit, swivel our hips, and lower ourselves to the ground below, but we got across. Wet seats were the only ill effect of our new crossing place. (Of course, had we gone barefoot like the villagers, we could have simply walked across, taking care not to let the unruly water knock us down.) Even if we had fallen, the sun was out and the air warm; we would not have stayed wet long.

It was too muddy to do much but inspect the farmers' crops and compost piles, but we were pleased to see that the rain had left some of the dryest piles looking as soggy as the rest of the world. To any farmer who would listen we explained that the sun would again beat upon them and build their heat to where it should be, and the bacteria planted in them by the animal dung would have its chance to multiply, prosper, and produce good loam.

In spite of the great mud balls gathering on our feet, we decided to walk to the far side of the village to follow up on a new lead. The meeting of the women's association in Gowa had given us such good contacts that we had tried to set up a similar meeting in Godino. But it was only at the end of the Godino meeting, made desultory by a number of passive male listeners from the farmer's association, that one promising moment occurred. Word reached Asellefech that the twenty-two-year-old head priest of the Godino Coptic Church might be interested in working with us.

Now, on this muddy morning, we thought we might confirm that idea by finding this young man. His name was Kafalaigne, and his tukel was the large, new one we'd noticed at the top of the village. To get to it we had to cross a field where our shoes collected huge balls of mud again. I became expert at kicking the mud from my feet every few steps. At least I had high plastic boots; Asellefech had only canvas slippers. With Asellefech's even temperament, however, few things were unremitting disaster. We made a game of mud-shaking until we finished off that field.

We arrived at the huge tukel and found its wooden door fast shut. The padlock and its hinge hung open, however, so we knocked. A young girl, barefoot and pregnant, opened the door. She confirmed that her husband, Kafalaigne, wanted to learn our vegetable growing methods. He was away at the church, however, but might be home that afternoon. We arranged to brave what we hoped would be a drier field and return.

Going home, we had to pick our way carefully along the village paths to stay out of the deep mire. Eyes glued to the ground, I had a brainstorm. Cows and donkeys deposited enough dung on the path that if I brought a plastic bag in the afternoon, I could readily collect a bulging supply for Dinkenish or Kenani. Neither had cows to furnish the dung she needed for her compost pile. Those who have cows use dung for fuel. Using their hands, the women mold it into patties about ten inches across, pile it, dry it, and burn it when they need a fire. Since they are also short of the green matter needed to nourish bacterial action in their compost piles, dung is needed to set the process in motion. But because they use dung for fuel they hesitate to put it in their compost piles. By collecting dung from the paths, could we start a new conservation effort?

We came to a mire in the path where cows had been herded through a large, low-lying puddle. We would need to thread our way along the high side of the path, pressed in by an acacia-thorn fence, to avoid stepping in the churned mud. We paused while an old, bearded man approached us, stepping cautiously around the edge through the mire with his sandaled feet. His walking stick was as gnarled as the bony hand that gripped it. We waited, watching his frail turban-headed figure move around the mud-patch. The horse-tail fly switcher he carried swayed with him. His progress was so slow that two young girls paused behind us, also waiting. Asellefech whispered, "He's ninety-three years." His age was common knowledge in Godino. A young farmer working just on the other side of the acacia fence looked up, saw four women waiting, and joshed, "Where you going, uncle?"

"To the village to beg."

"Should I kidnap a woman to take care of you?" the farmer quipped.

"No," the old man croaked, "I'm too old for women."

"What'll you do, then?"

"Go to church . . . pray to St. Mary. She'll take care of me."

The village of Godino watched over this man, their oldest kinless citizen, but their sense of burden was as playful as the light in his ancient, bleary eyes.

On the way back to Kafalaigne's that afternoon, even before I reached the stream, I had already collected a full, gooey, plastic bag of dung. We met Girme, the agricultural agent, on the path to Dinkenish's. He glanced at what I was carrying and said, "You really work hard, don't you." Playfully I told him I was fostering a new process for the village—making useful the ready-to-hand useless. Asellefech and I chuckled as we walked on and I explained to her that I felt like what Americans call a "bag lady."

That afternoon we found Kafalaigne at home. Clearly, here was a young man as ambitious to become a productive farmer as he was to be the chief priest. As we measured two very long beds, he described how his last year's teff crop had brought 3,000 birr. This year, he explained, he wanted to diversify his crop and figured vegetables were the way to do so. He did not work alone; a turban-headed old man helped him in the field. His mother and new wife also hung about to be helpful, but his fields evidenced the industry of his own efforts.

His mother voiced the same suspicions we had heard many times before. Would we not demand part of the crop produced from the seeds we had furnished? No, we answered wearily. They were his to keep.

After we'd measured his beds, Kafalaigne walked with us across the village to borrow a better pronged digging fork to do his double dig. Tadese, we knew, was finished with the one we had lent him. While we walked, Asellefech helped me ask Kafalaigne about his duties as the chief priest of the

Godino Coptic Christian Church. At twenty-two, this olive-skinned, handsome young man had been a priest since he was fifteen. He had begun to read voraciously about religious matters while still young, he said. Now, as the chief priest, his duties were to manage the affairs and ceremonies of the church. Hearing this story, I speculated that Godino might not have produced a Mozart, but it had produced a child genius in the form of a priest.

Kafalaigne dug two long double digs, preparing his beds faster than practially any farmer we worked with. Almost everyone who dug a double dig complained that it was hard work. Kafalaigne acknowledged the work, but he claimed the tool we had lent him made it easier.

The day we planned to plant, Kafalaigne was called away suddenly. We arrived with carrot seeds and found him gone, having delegated his wife and mother to plant in his place. He hoped, his mother said, we would come back the following day to explain to him about composting. His wife clearly wanted to make an occasion of our return—she trusted us now, she said—and promised to prepare coffee.

The next day, when we took out our sheet to explain the principle of composting and saw how Kafalaigne listened intently, we knew we had found an unusually ambitious contact farmer. He was determined to prosper, and had decided our methods might foster better crops. His gusto especially shocked me when we went to collect greens for his heap and Kafalaigne slashed mercilessly at a clump of lily-like flowers next to his vegetable field. Since there were so few flowers in the village, I stood watching regretfully until I remembered that these flowers grew from a bulb and would probably not suffer from being cut back.

When Asellefech and I were ready to stop piling green matter and manure on his compost, Kafalaigne was not. He wanted to go on, make it huge. We demurred. After the coffee that his wife had promised, we had other places to go. But we could see that this man wasn't dependent on our help. He would go on building the pile on his own.

Inside, Kafalaigne's wife offered us coffee complete with amenities: sugar, green grass on the tray, and incense. Kafalaigne sat formally on the smooth, dried-mud bench far from his wife's clay stove. He told us he had originally planned to build this huge tukel as a place to store his large crop of teff. However, the elders in his church had suggested that his fellow Christians might not approve of a priest who was single and so much wealthier than the other villagers. They insisted he get married and live more like other people. As he told us this I thought of what I had read about African village philosophy: individual interests were considered self-indulgent; what mattered was the well-being of the collective unit. I thought also of a conversation I had with another African about the African sense of community. He said, "You in the West get your sense of identity from Descartes. You say, *I think, therefore I am.* We in Africa think another way. We say, *We are, therefore I am.*"

Kafalaigne had taken the advice of the elders and found a wife. The way he told his story, however, made me curious about what he thought about women. Another clue came when he was unwilling to have his picture taken inside his home near the stove and beside his wife as she worked. Instead, he asked me to take a picture of him sitting on the opposite side of the tukel with his wife standing beside him.

His mother, invited by his wife, joined us while we were drinking coffee, but she stayed tentatively near the door. She listened intently, and before we left asked that we help her do a double dig. Her husband had died several years back, but she thought she would be able to dig a short plot herself. We left promising to be back to help her select a spot. When we did return we measured a plot, but she put us off for a week, for she was going to be busy preparing food for one of the Coptic ceremonies and had no time to dig.

On the way home that day, reflecting about Kafalaigne's uneasiness at being photographed in a working posture near his wife, we speculated that it might be my prestige as a foreigner that gave Kafaliagne the confidence to be "caught" alone in the presence of several women.

On another wet morning when work was slack, we called on Dinkenish. She asked if we could stay long enough for her to make coffee. Thinking her family could not afford coffee, we had hoped simply to relax with her, but we were delighted to be offered coffee, and she sent for Kenani to join us. Tadese was already at home, and Kenani joined him leaning against the tukel's center partition. Asellefech and I settled on a goatskin with our backs to the tukel's outside wall. Usually men were scarce during the times we gathered to speak with the women in Godino, but those who were around, with the exception of Kafalaigne, showed no uneasiness at being caught in women's company.

We sat speaking casually about the carrot, beet, and cabbage crop they expected to have, while Dinkenish roasted and pounded the coffee. "Do you know how to cook carrots?" I asked. Dinkenish had an idea—she would try to cook them as she did sauces for eating with injeera. Then Kenani turned flip. "Me? I haven't a clue," was the gist of what she said.

On the way home an idea came to us. Why not have a carrot and beet cooking party? The seeds we had planted in the village gardens were not ready to harvest yet, but in our demonstration garden we had full-grown carrots, beets, and beet greens. We could arrange a party, invite all the women who were growing vegetables, cook the vegetables in a sauce to be eaten with injeera, and give them an actual taste test. We knew the food would be good, but the villagers didn't.

Whether it was the party or what they might learn, all of the women were enthusiastic. Dinberie agreed to hold the cooking session under the leaf-covered trellis in her courtyard. We promised to bring the wood for the fire, the vegetables, and the injeera. A week before the party we went around the village inviting sixteen women with whom we'd worked; the day before the party we returned to remind thirteen of them.

188

It was those women who showed up in party attire at Dinberie's house that afternoon. We had asked them to bring knives so that everyone could have a part in cutting up vegetables, and Kenani brought a charred and battered thin metal pan for cooking.

The mood was gay as we sat on the low, dried-mud bench circling Dinberie's vine-covered courtyard. About five of us at a time peeled carrots and cut onions. All of us felt cheerful in spite of our onion tears, and Dinkenish and Kenani, who knew each other best, clearly felt both bawdy and playful. While I sat, tears running down my cheeks from peeling onions, Asellefech suddenly reported in English, in a tone that just barely concealed her shock, "They're talking about their vaginas!" Afraid to dampen the mood by a lot of talk in a language the women didn't understand, I didn't ask her until after the party what they'd been saying. She told me that Kenani had kidded Dinkenish about squatting so near the ground by the fire. Her vagina, Kenani insisted, dragged so low she'd probably lost it! Dinkenish had defended herself. "No I haven't. It's still attached to me!"

The party had a center, the cooking fire, and we all had a part to play around it chopping onions, peeling vegetables, collecting the scraps for compost. At one point, when I looked around the circle of thirteen women, five of us were peeling and cutting and two women had begun to blow on the fire. Ambasu's wife, Matakya, had come early to help us gather brush to get the fire going, and then had settled into the circle to hold and nurse her baby. Everyone but Wode seemed to feel at home. She had come in her usual green dress, but she cut no vegetables and seemed restless. I wondered if, since she liked men so much, she didn't particularly enjoy the company of women. After staying perhaps fifteen minutes she left, arranging with Almaz, who was present and taking an active part in the cooking, to call her when it was time to eat. Zeynash's daughter, Abubavitch, came early. Her mother, she said, would come later, since she was uncomfortably large with her child.

The first sauce we cooked had beet greens, onion, and a bit of tomato. Dinberie cooked it, squatting beside the fire to stir it steadily. The other sauce was made of finely cut carrots and beets together with less onion. Abubavitch and Almaz took turns stirring it.

When the smoke rose and bothered people's eyes, I asked Asellefech to tell them about the English proverb, "Smoke follows beauty." Hearing the translation, Dinkenish straightened regally to reign over us. "That's it," she said, "the smoke's in my eyes because I'm the most beautiful woman here!" With her protruding gums and gapped teeth, she knew she was far from the most beautiful woman there, but such was her sense of self that she could joke about her looks.

Midway in the party Sisay swept in, having walked the 13 kilometers from school in Debra Zeit. Thirteen women gathered in his courtyard couldn't discombobulate him! He joined us and took Mekdes on his lap to amuse her, making sure she kept out of the way of the fire.

When both sauces were cooked, all the guests, including Sisay, retreated inside to sit around two small wicker tables on which we set two trays loaded with injeera and the sauces. Everyone ate, one hand in her lap, skillfully tearing the injeera and picking up the sauce on it with the other. Being nowhere near as adept as Ethiopians at one-handed eating, I sat only briefly to sample each sauce. I preferred to hold the pot of cooked sauce and dish it out for the others in large dollops with a wooden spoon. When they had finished there was neither a scrap of injeera nor a drop of sauce left on either of the two trays.

On the way home Asellefech and I felt drunk with our success. Asellefech admitted that she was glad I had insisted we have the party before I left, because although she had intended to do it, it was more fun to do it together. Beriso, when he heard about our good time, asked that we repeat the party with Ann and Senbet in Gowa. Those families, he figured, would hear about it and not want to be left out. We did have a Gowa party, but since I didn't know those women as well, it was not as exciting for me as it was for Ann. When both parties were over, I decided I didn't care if these families ever ate carrots or beets again. The "promotion" parties were worth doing for themselves alone.

Another kind of deadening rain fell on us during the first weeks of March. At that time Jack and I roused early to loll in our sleeping bags listening to the 6:30 BBC morning news. Senbet in the next tent had a radio, which we heard through the tent walls. On Senbet's boom box the English-accented radio voice faded in and out—the batteries growing weak—but it appeared that the tension of the Gulf War might be over.

At the same time, however, the news our Ethiopian teammates heard in Amharic told of increasing tension: The Ethiopian Civil War was heating up. The Eritrean and Tigreyan rebels had advanced far enough to threaten Addis Ababa. Our Ethiopian campmates heard that news without alarm. They claimed that a year ago the rebels had threatened Addis. This push was only a repetition of an offensive that had been turned back once and probably would be again. It was only the foreigners who wondered what we were doing remaining so close to trouble.

Hearing this rain of unsettling news taught me something about myself. Until it actually happens, I seem unable to believe that anything bad can happen to me. When we were all mildly panicked and others looked to Jack and me for comment, for my own assurance I made up a scenario. "Suppose the rebels do take over in Addis Ababa. We're way out of any crossfire that might happen in Addis. If we were in an area the rebels took over, the probability that they would go after foreigners is less likely than that they would arrest Ethiopians loyal to Mengistu. They might well close the airport, and we would have a problem getting out, but. . . ." My scenario, I recognized, projected an unlikely rationalism. I knew that any chaos that might occur with a breakdown of government could hardly be faced rationally. But still we felt helpless and needed comfort. If what gave us assurance was naïve, so be it.

Personally, I had another hidden agenda, probably both callous and unrealistic. If something difficult did happen, as long as I didn't actually lose my life I would have collected another story to tell.

It was the Ethiopians I really worried about, since they were certain to be worse off if the war stepped up. Mengistu's renewed demands for more and more soldiers made the village still more tense. They all feared being forced to join the army and go to the front.

The rumor was that the rebel forces were radical communists and looked to Albania as their model for Communism. That was surely no outcome to think of as liberation! It might mean that Ethiopians chafing now under the yoke of the present government could hardly look to a new rebel government to rid themselves of Communism. One tyranny might replace another!

The next alarming barrage of news rained on the Soviets: The Soviet military and government advisers were pulling out of Ethiopia. Soviet air bases and advisory operations were expensive, and the USSR no longer had money for them. Our Soviet volunteers wondered if they should leave camp early. The U.S. Embassy added to our discomfort by suggesting that all U.S. non-essential personnel leave Ethiopia. Still, we could not believe that our rural setting 60 kilometers south of Addis would be attacked.

15.
The School:
"Am I Fat? Yes, You Is"

YEARS ago—was it in the photo collection *The Family of Man?*—I saw a picture of African children that embedded itself in my imagination. Showing five or six young boys at play, it caught half of them in the air and the others poised on the ground, knees bent, ready to shoot up. The energy of that game leapt from the page to mold my image of African children: ebullience and extraordinary verve.

Of the few books available to read while we lay sweltering in the early afternoons, one was David Lamb's *The Africans*. In it Lamb observes that African children tend to be precocious. He suggests two reasons for this: a child is strapped to its mother's back during the first year of life; that same child is left to its own devices at about age three.

I was curious to test this with Godino children. When we walked about the village paths, children often joined us. Even when Asellefech was with me to translate, some of them tried to communicate with single words and labored signs. Some were shy, some brash. Still, we communicated. When they showed off with brassy singing or by making their shoulders vibrate in a dance, it was exciting.

When Ann and I began to teach regularly in the school, however, I was able to experience the Godino children as individuals. After the winter holiday, I broke off work each Tuesday and Friday morning to act as an aid to the sixth-grade English teacher.

Not every village had a school. The one in Godino served at least four villages, but most of its students came from Godino and Gowa. A 1989 survey found that only 34 percent of primary-school-age children in Ethiopia were enrolled in schools. In addition, twice as many boys as girls were enrolled in primary and secondary schools. Children don't go to school as part of their fight to survive. Rather, if a family's fight to survive is not all-consuming, its boys, and sometimes its girls, may go to school. I had read David Lamb's observation that education in Africa is an end in itself, not a quest for broad knowledge, and I wanted to see this for myself.

Seven people made up the school staff and on our first visit I sensed that the teachers at Godino as well as the school's director, Aklilu, and its assistant director, Asmara, cared deeply about raising the quality of rural life in Ethiopia. When I went to teach, I usually arrived before class time at the open door of Aklilu's office, and was always invited to sit inside on one of the three rickety wooden chairs. If Aklilu was in the middle of some formal meeting, I sat listening to the Amharic, picking out certain words I knew. If another teacher was there and the talk was casual, they switched and chatted with me in English. I was charmed by the informality of my reception and convinced that even had I understood Amharic, they would have readily received me into their formal discussions.

Aklilu's wife, Tsaada, one of the two women teachers, was a favorite of mine. She was taller than most Ethiopian men, large-boned but slender, and one of the few Ethiopian women other than Asellefech whom I saw wearing slacks. Her English was good enough that whenever she was in the office we chatted. Once she told me she was eager that our work with the farmers include suggestions about child-rearing and health. I explained we weren't trained to help with those issues, but she insisted that our everyday common sense was what the women needed, and extracted a promise that in the course of teaching agricultural methods I would add what I could.

Educational amenities—athletic equipment, bright posters or maps for the walls, even books—were nowhere in evidence. A globe—an eighteen-inch miniature of the world—was kept high on top of one of the metal office cupboards and carried to classes only on special occasions. The only other map I saw was a huge map of Africa painted on the outside of the cement-block wall of the building beside the playground.

Tsaada's curiosity was expansive. She asked about American schools, and one day she asked that we locate the homes of each of the foreign volunteers on the globe. Like the other teachers, she taught a variety of subjects: reading, arithmetic, geography, and English. Her students were one of the younger groups, although I often saw her out under the trees in the schoolyard, supervising a group of older children while they wove baskets. I needed minimal translation when I taught, but I was never asked to teach unsupported by another teacher. Once, when Zellekech, the teacher I assisted, was absent, Tsaada eagerly left her class to come and join me.

One Saturday morning Tsaada walked by Zeynash's corner garden where Asellefech and I were planting cabbage seedlings and asked if we would come for coffee at her house down the way. Saturday mornings were always a bit slower paced as we rolled up to the weekend, and we were happy to think about relaxing when we finished. I had forgotten that Tsaada's husband, Aklilu, might be at home.

When we walked into their tiny living room, Tsaada was pounding the coffee into a powder, and the school director lolled shirtless like a courtesan in a back corner on a day bed. Wearing nothing but pants and a white cotton shawl that lay draped over his rich brown chest, he greeted us without rising. Tsaada seated us on two rickety wooden chairs beside a table under the room's only window.

The talk soon turned to the leafy branch of *chat* lying on the day bed beside his bare chest. From time to time Aklilu broke off a sprig and slipped it into his mouth to chew. "In your country," he asked, "have you narcotic like this?" I told him about marijuana. He decided the two were comparable. He told us chat was illegal—widely used in private, but seldom in public. When he used it, it had only a moderate effect on him. Now he was gleaning its highs on a bored Saturday at home. I remembered he had told me he preferred his responsible life at school to the empty weekends at home, and wondered if his current posture might help explain that preference.

While Tsaada went on preparing and serving the coffee, we all spoke about U.S. cultural life as compared with Ethiopian cultural life—a topic about which I sensed few other persons in Godino were well enough informed to speak. I left feeling the village was as isolated for this couple as it was for me. Also, I wondered, would Aklilu chew an opiate at home if he and Tsaada had children? Their childless house seemed empty and a bit lifeless, even to me.

At the heart of my zest for teaching in Godino were the children in the sixth grade. It wasn't that they were model children—they whispered and giggled regularly. It was their eagerness to have me teach them that was so captivating. Always when I walked into their cement-block classroom, they snapped to their feet. "Guh mornee, teechah." Forty-six eager brown faces and white-toothed grins greeted me. "Good morning, class. You may sit down." Always, I exaggerated my enunciation. They settled, four and five students to a bench behind a desk that would better hold two or three. "Turn to page 105." Zellekech always indicated which lesson she wanted me to prepare and go over orally. I aimed to have the children repeat everything in chorus after I'd said it. If they read the English words in their books at the same time, the sounds might stick better.

Their English book lessons were straightforward: "This is a notebook. . . . I speak English." We always practiced pronunciation in chorus for a period. When the chorus fell flat, as it always did when they grew tired, I moved out around the class to ask individual questions. Holding up a pencil, I might ask, "What is this?" The answer was almost always muttered shyly, but I usually got some version of "It is a pencil."

I frequently used one question from the book that elicited both speculation and giggles: "What do you want to become?" Sometimes I invited them to begin the answer in chorus: "I want to become a. . . . " Then I encouraged them to split off for the specifics. Their aims ranged from farmers to teachers to doctors to mothers. When the girls answered, "I want to become a mother," something niggled me into suggesting they add an adjective: "I want to become a good mother." Most students wanted to become farmers or teachers. One boy and one girl said they wanted to become doctors. One lone boy who was usually crouched against the wall in the front instead of sitting on the benches with others figured how to say brightly,"I wan to becuh a e-jin-eer."

When I taught high school in Seattle I observed that the students who had long-term career goals, even if they later altered them, seemed to have an easier time wading through the nitty-gritty and humdrum aspects of school work. Here there were whole shovel-loads of nit and grit and much grueling rote-learning ahead for any child who continued his education long enough to approach a profession.

The older boys—the fifteen- and sixteen-year-olds sitting five and six to a bench at the back of the class, were the most reluctant to mimic my pronunciation. Not, I guessed, because they knew any less English, but because their age made them more self-conscious about saying anything aloud. When I walked to the back of the class and cocked my head to hear them repeat after me, my closeness usually set off a panic. Then their chorus was ultra dead! One more reason to teach language early, I concluded.

I discovered that I could get this sixth grade class nearly shouting at me if I taught them short, easy-to-memorize, rhythmic jingles. To each new class I brought a different jingle and went back over the ones I'd already taught. At breakfast one morning Olga repeated a phrase she remembered from her English classes in a Moscow school. It went "Mother, father, sister, brother, hand in hand with one another." The Ethiopian sixth-graders adored it. The words were already familiar, and the rhythm and rhyme made the sounds fall out of their mouths easily. Another nearly nonsensical rhyme was "Roses are red, violets are blue, sugar is sweet, and so are you." I wasn't sure they knew what a rose was, and I was quite sure they didn't know what a violet looked like, but I was touched by their gusto in spouting the rhyme.

One day I passed a compound in the lower part of the village where a farmer was digging and noticed a vine climbing on his tukel that sported five or six blooming roses. A farmer prosperous enough to grow roses? Asellefech asked him if I could have just one. He walked to the vine, picked three, and wordlessly handed them over his thorn fence. His expressionless face made me wonder if he was proud or resented giving them to me, but I thanked him enthusiastically in Amharic all the same.

Half an hour later I arrived at school set to show my class the three roses I clutched, which had already begun to droop. Alas, another expectation dashed! They were destined to fade still further. There would be no class that day. The entire school was gathered outdoors in the courtyard for a program commemorating Ethiopia's victory over Italy in 1896. The program celebrated several battles in which Ethiopians pushed the Italian oppressors out of their country.

A single wooden table served as a podium around which the youngest classes sat in a semi-circle on the ground. The older classes stood at the back. In front of the students was a row of wobbly wooden chairs on which Negash, the medic, and the teachers were seated.

I arrived as Asmara opened the program, and was embarrassed when he paused in his speech to beckon to me.

I was to come from behind to sit at the front with my fading roses. The teachers vacated a chair for me. Another teacher rose and borrowed a straw hat from a boy lolling in the shadow of the building waiting to perform. They could not have me sitting hatless in the merciless sun, although several of the men wore no hat. All this settling in went on as if Asmara had not already begun to speak to introduce the program.

Once settled, I listened to Asmara read in Amharic from four worn pages held squarely in front of him. I heard the word "General" many times and guessed he was reading about the battle being celebrated.

Asmara finished, and the program continued with a series of readings—poems and essays read by the gym teacher and several students. A mock heroic delivery from each speaker emerged either dramatic or sing-song. After about an hour, the program picked up when six students, led by a fifth-grader named Saloman, burst forth dressed in feathered headdresses and armed with spears to re-enact with gusto a dance-like battle—Italians versus Ethiopians. The drama of the battle was complete with the lads' grunts. Clearly it was a bash to enact!

I had hoped the battle might be the climax of the program, but it dragged on. A young girl, dressed all in white with clean green cloth slippers, appeared before the table holding a shaking paper. She began to read, lifted her eyes just once to the audience, and nearly curled up in front of us from fright. Then she straightened, began again, and continued valiantly, keeping her eyes glued to the paper, ignoring her audience. We could scarcely hear her trembling voice, but she finished. I wanted to pass her the drooping roses. It was well past the time the students were due to go home for lunch, but the program showed no sign of concluding.

Bekele, Negash's nephew, was the star of the next item. He read an essay he had written about the battle, then led out a coterie of boys and girls to sing and dance three modern numbers while he improvised a musical background with a small bamboo pipe he'd made. The drum made the dancing lively, but nothing could revive either the rose or my flagging spirits. We had been sitting for an hour and a half in the hot sun. I was hungry.

After three more numbers, Aklilu approached the table, and in a soft voice brought the program to a limp close. I jumped up, elated, thrust the crumpled roses into Zellekech's hand to show the sixth-graders that afternoon, passed the hat back to its student owner, and sped home to lunch. Ann, who had arrived late and remained at the back, joined me. The usual cluster of children hurried with us. The program had been an intriguing curiosity, but I was glad to be moving rather than sitting under the merciless sun.

One day during class Aklilu slipped into the classroom and stood with Zellekech to listen. The lesson was on various words having to do with weight. "The elephant is heavy. The young boy is fat." We practiced in chorus until the tone went flat. Time to leave the printed page. Spontaneous speech, listening, and understanding skills were what these students needed.

I moved into the aisle between the benches. "Are your desks heavy?" I asked. In chorus came the answer. "Yes it is." I corrected them. "Yes they are," for the plural.

"Am I fat?" I asked. The chorus hesitated. I had trapped them. They had to make a vital decision. The need to be correct wiped out any sense these children might have of my playfulness. They had understood my question, but I saw in their faces the fear of answering wrongly.

Finally one brave child, speaking solo, said, "Yes . . . you is."

Some other more exacting spirit said, "Yes, you are!"

Zellekech and Aklilu looked on and chuckled. I got a mild shock. Even though while in camp I had lost some twenty pounds, by Ethiopian standards my size 14 was fat!

"No, you aren't fat," I taught the chorus to say. Alas, it was false flattery.

The teacher who taught agriculture at the school—it was

an elementary school subject—was named Zeynebe. Since that name means "rain," the myriad Ethiopians called Zeynebe may indicate something about the way that country feels about the blessing and power of rain. Asmara and Zeynebe were intrigued with setting up an experiment in the school garden, comparing the way carrots grew in a single dig twelve inches deep to the way they flourished in a double dig twenty-four inches deep. The first team together with the school children had made a long compost pile and dug the long beds. They needed to be planted, and we set up a schedule. A group of some twenty children and teachers gathered at the school's garden each time we put in new seeds: first carrots, then beets, finally cabbage seedlings.

The first cabbage seedlings that had been transplanted into the school plot were found the following morning burned out in the cracked earth. We had mistakenly put them in at eleven in the morning for the sun to beat upon. I arranged, then, to return with Ann the following Monday to replant just before the sun went down at five. The new seedlings might survive if they had the cooler night to settle in.

That Monday, having finished our transplanting, we started home, weary. Three boys and five girls walked with us, intending to bring back water from the stream. One of the small boys lugged our watering can, and three of the girls brought plastic jugs to carry the water, which would come from the village's only "clean" water source.

I moved slowly, weary at the end of a long day. Two of the girls began to sing and clap. The others joined in. The girls began beating their jugs in rhythm as if they were drums and moving at a dancing pace to the singing. Their spirit caught me up and I moved faster. Suddenly, new energy ran through my body down to my mud-caked jeans (I had taken a spill into an irrigation ditch on the way to school that afternoon), and I found myself shaking my shoulders. My companions moved faster and faster, singing lustily in a brassy chorus. One girl, an expert, added to her movements the quirky rapid shoulder shaking of Ethiopian dance. Down the dusty path we flew, making noise, beating time, celebrating! Again, I shook my shoulders, ineptly. They giggled and elbowed each other. This older foreigner—some strange bird! I lifted my chin, no longer so weary, and laughed. A memorable moment—dancing with the children of the world!

I advertised my final class on the day before our last day in camp as prize day. If they studied hard and could show me they'd learned their lessons well, they would each get a prize. Ploughshares had suggested that we bring small mementos to leave with the village, and this seemed the perfect time to distribute them. Carefully, I counted out my prizes: balloons, lapel pins, trinkets. Several of them might be elaborate enough to become "grand" prizes. Our teammates, who also wanted to bid the children and teachers goodbye, planned to arrive at school just as Ann and I finished our classes to join in the party atmosphere.

I arrived early. When I went in the teachers' room, Zellekech was not there, but Tsaada was. It was a good time to surreptitiously give Tsaada a special gift, a pair of cloisonné earrings. A friend in England had given them to me and I was fond of them, but I could see they would be infinitely more rare and beautiful in Godino. Tsaada, whose ears were already pierced, was delighted and put them right on.

Several of the sixth-grade boys stood in the open door of the teachers' room waiting for me, so Tsaada decided to go in with me to begin the prize day. A head start would help, since all the individual quizzes I had planned would probably take longer than the ordinary class period.

The first step: to enlist Tsaada in explaining to the students that I was going to go around the class, speaking the first word of a jingle. Each student was to finish saying it to win a prize. By this time I knew each child well enough to gauge which ones could handle the more complicated rhymes, and which ones needed the easy ones. I strode out into the middle rows and stared in the eyes of a young girl who had always been eager. "Mother . . ." I began. She continued "Father, sister . . ." and finished the two lines shyly but adequately. I gave her her prize, a red balloon. I could see the young boy next to her trembling with fear, so I moved across the aisle to another young boy who had also looked eager. "Roses," I began. "Are red . . ." he continued. And so I went through the class, waiting patiently while they stumbled out their phrases, prompting when it was called for, letting them romp when they were able.

When all forty-six students had earned a prize—some sat with round balloons in front of them, others with small lapel pins shining before them—I still had nine prizes left. How to distribute them?

Speedily, I improvised an elimination game to let them compete for the rest. Zellekech had taken over from Tsaada by that time, and I asked her to explain that we would now begin a game to win extra prizes. Those students who volunteered would come to the head of the class, and I would ask each of them a question. If they answered it in correct English, they would remain standing and move to the other side, the winner's side of the classroom. If they could not answer it correctly, they would go back to their seats. The winners would continue to answer questions until everyone had been stumped and one person remained to win the prize.

"Who wants to play?" Some twenty eager hands shot up. The older boys in the back were too cautious to expose themselves, but there were plenty of eager younger boys and some girls who wanted another prize. I pointed to five boys and five girls and asked them to come to the front of the class. When they stood in a straight line, fidgeting, I began. "Can you read Amharic?"

"Yes, I can." If they answered the question in a grammatically correct manner, they got to stay in front of the class and move to the victory side. "Does your teacher speak English?"

"Yes, she . . . do."

"Sorry," I hesitated, wanting to be gentle, "you must go back to your seat." Grinning, undefeated, caught up in the fun of the game, each child in error returned to giggle with his or her seat-mates. Nine times many of the same children's hands shot up bidding to compete. Nine times I stumped them all down but one for the prize. They were never embarrassed or tired of the game, even in defeat.

On the tenth round the question stumped them. "Do monkeys speak English?" They tried everything. "No, he can't," "Yes, I can," The closest was "No, he don't." No one was able to come up with the pronoun "They" to say "No, they don't." With this question eliminating so many children, they dashed up and sat down in rapid succession. Suddenly I recognized in the flurry of the fray I had run out of prizes! What to do? This, the toughest of all questions must surely have a reward!

Sergei and Vladik stood at the open door watching. The other foreigners had arrived; time was nearly up. Then Sergei, alerted, recognized my problem. Deftly he reached to his lapel, removed a pin that symbolized the Soviet Peace Fund, and handed it to me for a prize. Eureka, I was saved!

I continued the game. But no one could answer correctly! Finally, I changed the question to award the prize. "Do you eat injeera?"

"Yes, I do." the young girl answered, and I had a pin to give her.

Elated by the times the children had tried and tried again and let themselves be stumped, when everyone had returned to their seats, rewarded, I repeated the king question. Say after me: "Do monkeys speak English? No, they don't!" A choral moan of recognition emanated from the entire class. Then a sing-song chorus began, with me conducting. It became a chant, "No, they don't; no, they don't; no they don't." Then I shouted "goodbye" and extracted myself. The uproar and chanting made it easier to hold back my tears when I thought that I would never again ask these delightful sixth graders "Do monkeys speak English?"

When I was home again, certain Godino children continued to dance in my memory—especially when I glanced in the mirror and asked, "Am I fat?"

"Yes, you is!"

That same afternoon, the day before our last day in camp, I longed for an equally up-beat atmosphere in which to say goodbye to Tsaada. She had asked me to stop by her house to pick up a basket the children had made in the handicraft class for Pam Bauman, who had ordered and paid for it.

Asellefech and I stopped for a final coffee, and Tsaada gave me a bright, woven bread-basket of yellow, green, and red, the Ethiopian colors. As we left her house, telling her we had a few more fourth-grade girls' gardens to check, Tsaada said she and the other teachers would be over at camp in half an hour. We wondered why. We'd already said goodbye so many times that my forced cheer was fading.

Later, when we reached home, we found Tsaada, Asmara, Aklilu, Zeynebe, and Negash sitting under the awning at our camp dining table with the other camp members— Soviet, American, and Ethiopian. Drawing closer, we saw that they had brought wine and Pepsi and that it was a party. Our Ethiopian teammates would not touch the alcoholic beverages, but they were no less warm than the rest of us as we tried to show these teachers how much we admired their work in the village.

We all sat for another half-hour talking and drinking. Aklilu described the pall he sensed had come over the school that afternoon when the children realized the foreigners were leaving. Finally, when Tsaada and I stood to say goodbye, there was a terrible fervency to our hug. Our two open personalities had touched a chord in each other. It would vibrate a good while.

16.
What Do You Do When There's Nothing to Do?

DURING our final days in Godino, as the camp work was grinding down, the war was heating up. Our morale buckled.

Nothing could be done to soften our fear and uncertainty about the war, short of leaving the country. We foreigners began to anticipate being trapped like rabbits with their exit holes sealed off if the rebels should reach Godino while we were still in camp.

We didn't like our cowardly inclinations, and clung to the hope that the rebels wouldn't reach Addis before we were scheduled to leave Ethiopia at the end of March. If they did, surely we'd be able to slip through Addis and out of the country. But nothing was certain.

Toward the end of our time in camp, those of us on the outreach team were finding more and more contact farmers in the villages, but those of the team left in camp had essentially worked themselves out of a job. The food-for-work Ethiopians were doing the regular farm work: tending the vegetables, planting fruit tree seedlings, and building with mud bricks. In camp, only odd jobs were left, if we were resourceful enough to create them. Sergei and Vladik decided there was no further work worthy of their efforts, which meant that Sergei launched a barage of complaints and lay on his bed most of the day, emerging only for meals. Vladik followed suit.

All the faranji felt cheated of the three sight-seeing trips our Ethiopian hosts had promised at the beginning. The Soviets were especially bitter. It was as if the gasoline shortage that had forced our trips to be cancelled were FSO's fault, not the fault of the situation in the country. The U.S. team members resisted attaching blame; nonetheless, we too felt the need for a break from camp.

In the privacy of our tent, Jack and I speculated that lack of funds for a trip, in addition to the fuel shortage, might be another of FSO's difficulties. When Roba, for FSO, had asked Ploughshares in Seattle not to send the third team scheduled to arrive April 1, we guessed that the planning for and the expense of foreign campers was becoming burdensome. What if we offered to pay for our own hotel and food? One evening around the candlelit table, we had a long and lively group meeting. After discussing all our options, the foreign volunteers offered to furnish the money for a trip, provided the hotel and food did not cost above 100 birr apiece—about $50. All FSO had to do was find a car with gas enough to take us to Awash Park.

At the meeting, Gitachew saw how much the group wanted a trip out of camp. The next day he went to Addis, got Roba's backing, and made extensive inquiries. But no car, no tourist bus, nor any form of transport could be found. When he returned and reported his failure, I sensed a suffocating force of anger directed at him at that evening meal. Most of our teammates, convinced that if Gitachew had tried hard enough he would have found something, wouldn't take his word that he had tried. I believed he had, but I couldn't quash my own disappointment. Once again, Gitachew had been ineffective as our supply person.

Belay got word of our low morale and wiggled loose from his Addis work to briefly turn up in camp. He announced that FSO and the Soviet Embassy were planning a bang-up "closing ceremony." If anticipation of such a celebration was meant to lift our spirits, it didn't! Ceremonies might be good public relations for FSO, but we considered them dull and a waste of money.

Belay's reading of our morale must have confirmed that some kind of final trip for us had to be arranged. He returned to Addis, and immediately the word came that FSO thought they could put aside at least enough gas to take us to Soderi, a hot springs some 70 kilometers to the south. *Whoop-te-doo!* A plan was made. We would spend the night at a hotel in Nezareth. As a group, we would get out of camp and have a good time!

The ever-cheery Abebe drove us to Soderi hot springs. Sitting next to him I observed how he often cut off the engine at any tiny incline. Even on the level, he drove until he was going fast enough to cut the motor and coast to a slow pace before he kicked the motor in again. A master driver and mechanic, and a master at saving gas! On that trip the van was packed full with eight foreign campers, plus a food-for-work worker and Senbet traveling to visit their families in Nezareth. Until we reached Debra Zeit, where we dropped Asellefech, we were especially heavily loaded.

Jack and I were seated in the van's front seat, and riding beside Abebe, we could chat with him. Only twenty-nine years old, he was excited about the recent birth of his sixth child, a girl. In spite of his boundless enthusiasm for her beauty, he insisted this daughter would be their last child. We learned, also, some new facts about Abebe's country. It was his opinion that Ethiopia had many untapped resources, including oil. The government, however, had been so distracted by the war that all beneficial development had been stalled.

At an unimposing gate to Soderi's park, we stopped to pay a stiff entrance fee. As we drove in we passed two low, tree-shaded buildings. Holiday-spirited, wealthy-appearing Ethiopians relaxed on their verandas. Other folk ambled quietly along the road.

With this atmosphere, Soderi already offered a striking

contrast to camp life. Living and working in Godino I had begun to feel that all Ethiopians were as poor as those I knew in the village. I had also decided that although Godino villagers were poor, they didn't appear to suffer inordinately from their poverty. Was it because they hadn't seen enough of a wealthier life style to know what they were missing? Now I speculated that for their own endurance of their poverty, it might be a good thing Godinoites hadn't been to Soderi. This resort would give villagers a glimpse of an Ethiopian life style both luxurious and inaccessible to them.

The Ethiopians we saw vacationing had driven to the Soderi hot springs and were enjoying life in the middle of a tremendous gasoline shortage. There was no sign they felt the threat of the military collapse of their government. Everyone we observed seemed to be laughing and growing as fat as any Ethiopian ever gets. Loud-speaker music—western-style pop—pervaded the ambiance of the pool. Most of the resort's customers were younger Ethiopians. Some hung about in the parking lot joshing with their companions beside their Mercedes cars. Young girls loitered at poolside wearing svelt bikinis. (Never had I been in a nation so replete with beautiful women as Ethiopia.)

My own pool experience was overwhelming. It was the hottest water I have ever been swimming in. The temperature was a bit hotter than I like my baths. At first the water refreshed, since the day was hot, but to stay in and swim for longer than five minutes wilted me. What was pleasantest was to find a spot to loll in at a spot in the pool where a stream of water entered. To locate such a jetstream was like finding myself in a huge jacuzzi.

At poolside was a troop of monkeys padding about, frolicking, and begging for food from the bathers. Vladik spent most of the day charmed by and communing with the chattering creatures. At one point I happened to pass him, and he put a fist-full of peanuts into my hand. I began to eat them before I realized he had not given me the nuts to eat. He was inviting me to join him in feeding the monkeys from my hand. When I did, I marveled at their free-wheeling personalities. With their long arms they grabbed the peanuts I parceled out to them as if it were my privilege as a human to feed them.

Sun-bathing next to Olga, on the grass at the side of the pool, I batted the flies. "I will soon see my Alyosha," she said. "My husband writes Alyosha's teacher say he behaves badly. My husband is called to go to school two times already to talk to head teacher. It's time for me to be home with him." Suddenly, tears flooded Olga's eyes. "I did not know how much time away from home I was coming for. Sergei and Vladik, if they had not been my friends, I would cry every night in my tent."

As I, a mother, lay on that warm grass, I heard another mother speaking, and perhaps for the first time sensed Olga was a person with ordinary longings and needs. My sun-bathing companion had stopped being some symbolic "Soviet woman" and become real. The road she had taken to Ethiopia eagerly had turned out to be too long. Now she longed to retrace her steps.

"I want to thank you," I said, "for the new energy you've shown back in camp." I was referring to the fact that on her own during the past week Olga had observed that the hedges and beds in the camp itself (not just in the demonstration garden, where food-for-work workers did most of the work) needed weeding. With fierce resolve she had begun cleaning up. Then she had busied herself tidying every part of camp. She had asked Sergei to help her, but in those final weeks he was incapable of overcoming his disgust and inertia. He joined her for about ten minutes once a day before retreating to his bed in a sweltering tent.

We fell silent. Lying in the sun in this changed atmosphere at Soderi I reflected on our initial hopes for Soviet-U.S team work. I was disturbed by how things had turned out. Were the three younger Soviets part of the team? Now, at the end of camp, Noel and Ann, who spoke Russian, felt close to Ruslan and cut off from the other Soviets. Ann in particular was disgusted with Sergei; she could understand what he said, and found him shallow. Although Olga had knit a sweater for Asellefech and the two women were still tent-mates, our Ethiopian teammates had also, for the most part, written off all the Soviets except Ruslan.

Jack and Ruslan also brushed aside their inability to use words with each other, and found excuses to work together. They had grown immensely fond of one another.

Ruslan felt the Soviet Peace Fund had been unfair to him by appointing him leader of the Soviet delegation just before the Soviet team boarded the Aeroflot flight to come to Ethiopia. Particularly in the early weeks of our stay, he had assumed that role, but now at the end of the camp he was so disappointed with the other three Soviet volunteers, he had cut himself off from them almost entirely.

That attitude seemed unfair with regard to Olga. It made me try still harder to let her know how resourceful I thought she had been in finding a work project at the end of camp. I felt the others were not acknowledging how she had finally pulled herself away from Sergei's influence and, as a transla-tor and communicator, taken a more active and useful part in our group life.

During the final weeks of camp Vladik seemed to be withdrawing from the group, except for this trip. His with-drawal was exacerbated by an illness after the trip. The final week he spiked an erratic high fever. When Ruslan took him to Balcha, they diagnosed him as having some kind of undu-lant fever and kept him in Addis several days until he recov-ered. There was a possibility, it was rumored, that fleas from the monkeys he had been so charmed by at Soderi had bitten him and caused his fever.

All in all, however, our weekend trip and the night spent in that Nazereth hotel gave us a warmer feeling for each other. I began to compile a list of nicknames we could give each other at the closing ceremony.

On the way home from Soderi that Sunday evening we stopped off at ILCA to use the telephone. Ann called her

American relief worker friend in Addis and got disturbing news—he insisted the war situation was ever more precarious. He was not an alarmist, she said, but he had told her that if he were making the decision for her, he would instruct her to leave the country immediately. Each of us heard that report with varying degrees of anxiety.

How contrary to our early expectations were those final days in camp. It was not that we hadn't knit together as a group. We had. What's more, we had probably demonstrated what Ploughshares had hoped we would demonstrate: that Americans and Soviets can work together harmoniously in the third world. But most significantly, we had learned new things about ourselves. We were no working giants in utopia. Instead, we were more like nervous dwarves in a hellish corner of fairy-land. Still, despite all the irritations and some wrangling, we had formed a curious bond with one another. Some of us had connected and would continue to feel that way. Others of us were irritants we would be happy to slough off. Some of us were workers, some slackers. We had lived for a time as part of a miniature microcosm of the world. We had come out feeling more realistic about the world's possibilities. Unity in diversity was possible, but tough.

That last Sunday night in camp, Noel played the violin in his tent by candlelight. The incongruity of those clear string tones struck home. Ethiopia had confronted us with chaos, but this night we could still catch a scrap of beauty from those violin notes. Play out, violin! Schubert, if you can't sooth us, nothing can.

17.
The Village—
That's Where It Is

FTER our jaunt to Soderi, to be back walking to the village seemed as right as shedding mud-caked jeans and donning clean ones. Since we had been forced to forego the unique sights at Lalibella and Axum (they were in forbidden war zones), and because the countryside seemed so deadened by the war, sightseeing in Ethiopia hadn't felt right. Besides, we hadn't come to Ethiopia to sightsee. The village was where I wanted to be.

We worked that morning with the priest Kafalaigne's mother, measuring for her beds and helping her clear the refuse from a patch of ground near her small tukel. That afternoon on our way home, four fourth-grade girls—all in faded dresses and cotton slip-on shoes—waylaid Asellefech and me. While they explained their request I gazed at their clean faces and bright eyes wondering at the contrast with their loosely-braided and unkempt hair. I speculated that twisting and combing their hair must be difficult to do on their own, so that they don't braid their hair each day.

These girls had seen and learned from the experiment in the school garden; now each of them wanted a double dig. Would we come to their houses and look at the spaces they had to dig in? Their request, shy though it was, delighted us, since it was another sign we were gaining influence in the village.

That final week, then, our late afternoons were busy with fourth graders. In the U.S., to be busy after school with fourth graders might imply anything from a scout troop to some sport or musical activity. In Ethiopia, to be busy after school with these girls meant we might influence their very sustenance for their entire lives. Girls who stayed in school through the fourth grade were by that sign among the privileged and most forward-looking of the village people.

The following day we met one of the girls in the open market square. A new friend of the original four, her hair neatly braided and her dress torn at the waist seam, hurried to catch us and begged us to stop at her house as well, just off the market square where we were. As we detoured, I observed that there was no water nearby—the irrigation ditch ran its course on the other side of the village—and wondered if it mattered.

We made our way through two small, windowless rooms of the family's wood-and-mud shack to the back yard, where the fourth grader had persuaded her mother to let her dig a small garden just beside the thorny fence. Three of the other fourth graders appeared, and ten or so curious village children crowded into the tiny yard with us. The girl's mother, a small, big-eyed child clinging to her skirt, moved into the back yard to look on. Three neighbor women peered curiously over the back acacia-branch fence.

Proudly, the girl showed us the tiny garden bed she had already prepared. It lay perhaps three feet from the only latrine we'd seen in our three months in the village—an open pit covered by a torn, four-foot square sheet of rusty iron.

"I told her it was a terrible place to grow vegetables," the mother's high pitched voice complained, "but she wants to have what her friends have."

I picked up a longish stick and thrust it into the raised bed. The depth measured only twelve inches, not the twenty-four inches that a double-dig required. Asellefech explained how to dig the bed deeper, add sand and manure, and make it ready for the carrot seeds, which we promised to bring the next afternoon.

On our way back through the mud-walled house, I caught the eye of the girl's small brother. He stood, bare-bottomed and dressed only in a teal-blue baggy sweater, still clinging to his mother's skirt. He looked at me and shrieked! I smiled. He stopped shrieking for one fleeting smile, then began a long continuous wail. A white-skinned dragon had appeared before him. It was too much!

His sister explained apologetically that he had never seen a white person before. Hoping to quiet him, I hurried away into the front courtyard. Oddly captivated, the child followed, still whimpering. His sister, determined to guarantee that when we returned the next day there would be no more shrieking, grabbed her small sibling deftly by one arm and swung him onto her back. Then, with the child piggy-back, her two hands cradling his small bare bottom, she moved beside me to join the parade to her friends' houses. From the safety of his sister's back, the small boy looked at me curiously. I smiled, and there was no returning shriek. He even tried a smile.

The following day I got another reminder of the oddity of my white skin. When another girl's coffee-colored mother emerged from the house to see what we were doing, she carried a child whose light skin was nearly as pale as mine. I clucked at the child, and this touched off the mother's story: "One day you and your husband passed by here in a horse-cart. My friend and I saw you. My friend pointed to my baby and said, 'You're not the mother of that child—there goes its mother.'" I chuckled and assured the woman I was flattered, and I hoped she was.

As we worked in Godino that week, my mixed feelings about the camp's final days surfaced. I was ready to leave Ethiopia, but I dreaded saying goodbye. What was important was that the work in the village should and would continue, and I doubted all the energy FSO was putting into the preparations for the closing ceremony had anything to do with our basic work in Gowa and Godino. To cement the contacts we'd made was the only important "ceremony" to me.

The Friday before the closing ceremony, Asellefech and I walked to every corner of the village to say goodbye and to make it clear that Asellefech would continue to work in the village. We stopped at Sisay's and Dinberie's, and they insisted they had planned a more formal goodbye. Could Jack and I and Asellefech please return later that afternoon? We did.

Entering their courtyard, we found they had spread green grass and pink oleander flowers over their usually litterless inner court and sitting room floors. Clearly, they had planned something special. "Where did the flowers come from?" I asked.

"Your camp." Sisay said. In contrast to our western standards, his answer spoke of a certain sense of community property in the village. Why, I wondered, had I thought no one should pick flowers that did not belong to them?

Dinberie had prepared several things to eat. First she served the same thick sour milk she had served us before. When we had finished that, she brought out injeera and a cabbage sauce, or wat. Finally, she placed before us a basket with bananas from their own tree. While we were drinking the milk, Mekdes insisted she be allowed to spoon her milk out of the glass, since that was the way I did it. Her insistence was that much more noticeable since she was the only one of the family given milk. The others claimed they were still fasting and would not eat milk products until the Easter holiday.

Mekdes flirted unrelentingly with Jack, and he responded. That afternoon, in that tiny room, Jack ceased to be a big, bass-voiced man, and clucked in gentle tones with this tiny girl. Her brother, Aserat, had a banana, Jack had a banana, and Mekdes also had a banana. Each of them began to peel the banana and plainly, Mekdes was not practiced.

Jack joshed softly with her while he stripped his. As if they understood each other's language, the three-year-old giggled and taunted this strange man.

Dinberie then brought out an intricately woven basket patterned in soft reds, blues, and greens. I had seen similar but smaller baskets and others done in brash, loud colors. This one was a treasure. But when Dinberie handed it to me as a gift, Mekdes did not approve. She trotted to me, grabbed the basket, and took it back into the room behind the curtain. Her parents were embarrassed. "Did you make it?" I asked Dinberie.

"It was given to me as a gift, but you came and loved us and I want to give it to you," she said. Still, no words of contradiction, no struggle ensued with Mekdes. The basket remained in the back room until later. As we were leaving, Dinberie retrieved it from behind the curtain and gave it to me again. This time Mekdes was either resigned or did not see. She made no fuss.

Saturday, the day of the closing ceremony, dawned and Asellefech and I went off to the village early to see friends. We arrived back to find our camp changed. Our row of tents had become part of a shaded garden plot where white and black visitors strolled or clustered in twos and threes to talk. I, too, suddenly became a stranger in camp. Nonetheless I dove into our tent to change into a dress. I had worn a skirt in camp only twice before.

Dusty beneath my clothing, clean on the surface, I came out of the tent and chose to amble with a German relief agency official who had brought his wife. We headed toward the fish ponds, and while we wandered the quarter mile through the demonstration plot we could observe the vegetable beds. It seemed good to forget about the war in Ethiopia and speak about growing vegetables.

Beriso, still dressed informally in a clean khaki jumpsuit, lingered in his bright-eyed glory up by the fish ponds to show off the healthy cabbage heads and flourishing beet greens the fish had fostered. In English he explained to our guests that one of the villagers—it happened to be Zeynash's daughter, the one with a sick baby—could not wait until her own small crop of cabbage came to large heads. She had come to our garden, purchased 50 birr worth of cabbage heads, and transported them in a hired horsecart to Debra Zeit for selling in that city's market. This was the kind of initiative and self-reliance, he said, that we hoped to stimulate in the villagers with whom we worked.

Walking back to camp in the relentless sun, I found myself beside a gray-haired gentleman suffering under a suitcoat. As he wiped his brow with a white handkerchief, I commiserated with him with signs and simple language about the disaster heat made of formal dress. He introduced himself in excellent English. He was the newly appointed Soviet head of Balcha hospital.

"My stay will be too short in Ethiopia," he said, and I wondered at his regret in leaving this war-torn country. We talked of Ethiopian medical problems and their management given the current shortage of medicines. Then we compared Russian and American music. The heat beat upon my head and radiated up from the sun-cracked ground, but because the conversation intrigued me, I was able to ignore it.

We arrived back at the tent site and found that benches had been arranged in a horseshoe between the wash house and the row of tents. The benches at the top of the horseshoe were arranged beneath the Soviet, U.S., and Ethiopian flags—another alteration to the camp; since the first team's arrival last October, those solitary flags had hung on that high wire with nothing beneath them.

Now about twenty Ethiopian village men straggled in, grouped themselves, and settled beneath the flags for the program. Belay perched in their midst to whisper translation. When the meeting began, there was something I didn't like about that whispering translation. It was more important to me that these villagers understand and value our work than any foreigners, and yet for the foreigners there was spoken translation for which the speakers paused. I sensed the Ethiopians should also be given the honor of formal translation. But perhaps it didn't matter. The formal speeches, even the informal one I intended to give, didn't seem relevant to a villager's world. They sat with stolid posture and stony faces as if they did not care to hear Belay's whispered translations.

Ann had expected to be the main translator, but she had laryngitis. The strain to her voice was so evident that one of the English-speaking Soviet guests gallantly offered to relieve her. Noel was not available to translate; he had taken off for Gowa before the guests began arriving. "I couldn't stand the hypocrisy of being thanked for doing something they had kept me from doing," he told me afterward.

I, too, must have appeared another stony listener. Although I enjoyed chatting with the U.S. diplomats, I was not interested in the formal speeches the Soviet and American diplomats offered. I was also nervous at the thought of giving my "nickname" speech because it was so personal to the camp's life and so irrelevant to the guests. I looked about at the crowd. In spite of the gas shortage, FSO board members and Soviet and U.S. officials had arrived from Addis and formed an impressive row of five or six vans and jeeps lined up just inside the camp's gate. The Soviet volunteers planned to leave camp and return to Addis after the ceremony, and it appeared there would be ample transport for them to do that. The U.S. volunteers planned to stay on until Sunday morning. I clung to the idea that our goodbyes were important to the villagers and hoped to stage our leave-taking at a time when no unrelated dignitaries might be observing our simple expressions of fondness.

Jack had been asked to say something to represent Ploughshares. Ruslan would have had to speak for the Soviet Peace Fund, except that an official had arrived from the Soviet Union to open a hospital that the organization had remodeled in Debra Zeit. Ruslan, who was not the type for formal speech-making, had gotten himself off the hook by insisting that the official represent the Fund at both ceremonies.

When Jack began to speak I was startled out of my boredom. Here was his "punchy papa" side! He spoke openly about both the successes in the village work with contact farmers and the failure to find sustained significant work for the team in camp. I found his honesty refreshing. How might others find it?

I had little time to wonder, because suddenly it was my turn to give my nickname speech. As I moved to the front table to begin, my wobbly knees told me how uncertain I was. I began with a safe, innocent person. Senbet was our "lovable, furry-voiced Teddy Bear," and as I found him in the audience I saw him smile. I explained that the public's view of Senbet was of a young man who took considerable initiative with the village farmers and used his verbal facility to explain agricultural methods. Our view of him was more intimate. Something about Senbet always made me want to pet him.

Then I looked for Ruslan so I could watch him as I said he was our "Gold, Silver, Bronze Friend: gold for his warmth, silver for his humor, and bronze for his solidity." As I said this his face remained expressionless. When Ann's translation came through to him, his eyes lighted slightly. My name for him was a turn-about. Ruslan himself was always calling others of us his "silver friend" or "gold friend" in a joshing way to show his fondness for us. He did not josh with his female teammates, but he had other ways to let us know he respected us.

I called Ann "Energy Efficient," and to anyone whose mother tongue was not English I suggested that each of those words separately fit her. Her energy was abundant, and she was tremendously efficient. In the U.S., I explained, we considered the best kind of car to be "energy efficient." As Ann translated her own nickname, I looked at the villagers. They didn't get it. Their faces were no less stolid.

I dubbed Olga a "Creative Sleeper," noting that in

English someone who is slow to reveal their depth and ability is called a sleeper. I'd seen at the last how creative Olga was about finding work. When I saw that none of the non-Americans seemed to get my point, I decided to privately tell Olga of another connotation I had in mind for "sleeper." One evening at the table the team had discussed what each of us hoped to do in the next five years. Olga had said she'd been thinking about having another child. She wanted a girl. Picking up on that, I told her I hoped she would become a "creative sleeper" with her husband once she was back home. "What about creating a daughter?" I asked her.

Gitachew, who stood at one side, I labeled "King of Effort." He had, after all, often tried hard for us. His efforts frequently turned out to be fruitless, but he had always given us effort. He nodded graciously.

Noel's label was "Music First Noel," playing on the title of the Christmas carol. I recalled that Noel means "good news" in English. Noel had put music first and given us all calmer nights with his "good news" violin. I was sorry Noel wasn't in the audience to hear me, and resolved to tell him.

Even though Abebe was not an official team member, I thought of him as part of the team and called him "Ever-cheerful Charlie," or "Bubbling Abebe." The spunk of the English alliteration seemed to fit him.

Sergei's label was the most obvious. I called him "Goof Off." Aware, however, that should he hear the phrase and ask for a translation, I ought to be ready with something a bit softer, I had consulted Ann. Could she translate the phrase to take the sting out of it? Now as I spoke it seemed important not to hedge on the truth of these nicknames, but I couldn't bring myself to glance at Sergei to measure his reaction. "Sergei talks a good line, but he likes to party" was the phrase Ann hit upon in Russian. Clever Ann! When I finally glanced at Sergei, there was no change in his expression. I guessed it had worked to translate "Goof Off" as "he likes to party."

Jack I called "Punchy Papa" or "Battered Baba" to indicate that his usual mild manner under duress had gotten wilder, punchier. The audience had just seen one of his feistier sides in his speech. For Vladislav, I hit upon "Go Far Vladik" since I saw him as the one who was apt to achieve more than any of us. He had more time to get where he was going, after all, since he was our youngest. I was certain Vladik would later back up his ambition and skill with results.

Then there were the Ethiopian teammates I was closest to. Asellefech, seated on a bench between Senbet and Olga, listened without seeming to hear as I called her a "Gentle Dynamo." Few people in this crowd other than her teammates knew Asellefech, and probably only her teammates understood as I tried to make plain the paradox of my label. I felt her power over people was that much stronger because she was consistently energetic and gentle.

For Belay's label, I tried to put a gleam in my eye as I took a small dig at the FSO administration that had told us early in our visit that we were to look to Belay as our captain. They had reneged, I thought, by insisting that he remain in Addis during so much of our stay. We felt abandoned, and that translated into Belay's nickname: "Our abdicated, but certainly not vanished captain."

And Beriso? I peered out to the surrounding crowd. He didn't seem to be standing at the edge of the gathering where he had been. I wanted him there when I showed my fondness publicly. "Big Daddy" was my name for him. He was, after all, the person we looked to in the end for leadership. He was only thirty-six, but he had been like a father to us all.

I finished my labels and glanced at the villagers. There was no sign that they had understood any of it. Their stone faces had not changed. But it didn't matter. I took my seat and prepared for comments from my teammates who had understood.

The ceremony ended. We all rose happily and moved through the bougainvillea hedge. All of us—villagers, foreign and Ethiopian officials, and team members—could finally feast. Near the kitchen, four tables were laden with food.

Since Friday morning two goats had been tethered in the long grass near the kitchen to graze their last mouthfuls. A special goat-barbecuer had arrived early that Saturday morning to butcher and roast the animals for the feast. Our camp cooks had prepared what food could be readied ahead of time and stored without refrigeration—a small proportion of the offerings. The kitchen had been a-bustle since Wednesday. The kerosene for the kitchen's regular range-type stove had run out, but two charcoal braziers had burned almost constantly either inside on the cement floor or outside near the kitchen door.

Our moods picked up. The tables looked beautiful and bright. There was injeera and myriad vegetable wats and whole trays of cut fruit. The goat was barbecued to perfection, which in Ethiopia appears to include rubber-quality toughness. All was meant to be washed down with bottled Pepsi and boiled water.

We served ourselves. Wandosun and the cooks ran back and forth over the grass to keep the supplies on the tables replenished. I saw no Soviet vodka being consumed. Since we all ate without cutlery, off our knees or standing balancing our plates, there was considerable commotion but no surprise when someone's plate spilled and scattered on the ground. The camp dogs were called in briefly to share in the ground-feast, and the hapless gentleman, without chagrin, returned to the table for another heaping plate.

The highlight of the ceremony came privately for me. While eating, I was called aside because one of the food-for-work workers wanted to see me. When I found him, he stood with a woven-straw hat in his hands. A month back I had contracted with this gentleman to make me a hat, and I had given him several bits of colored yarn to work into the tightly woven sisal base of the hat. It was ready now, and it fit me. In exchange for it he wanted a pair of Jack's dilapidated old boots. Our Ethiopian teammates complained that in that barter I had vastly raised the price of woven hats!

As people were preparing to leave, Roba asked Asellefech and me to go to the village to help with a video film being shot at the homes and gardens of some of our contact farmers. Before we left, Sergei came to me and enthusiastically kissed my hand. He brought Olga to translate, and thanked me effusively for the nicknames I had given him and each of our teammates during the ceremony. Both astounded and relieved, I recognized Ann had succeeded in her translation. Either Sergei didn't understand the slur implied by the phrase "goof off," or he was too thick-skinned to feel the sting.

I didn't mind going off to the village before the Soviets left camp; we would see them again in Addis with almost a week to wait for the day our reservations would get us on planes—theirs to Moscow, ours to London. Now our farewells to the villagers were more important.

18.
Cemented:
By Simplicity? By Ironies?

WHILE Asellefech and I were tramping about the village with Roba and the cameraman, our Soviet teammates left camp. We came back from the village, and they were gone. Jack reported there had been no fanfare. They shook hands with the cooks and other Ethiopians they knew, climbed into the cars of the Soviets who had come to the ceremony, and drove off to Addis. Since I hadn't said a proper goodbye, I was happy we had planned a team dinner at a hotel in Addis for the following Thursday evening.

The fact that the U.S. and Soviet teams were leaving camp at different times, and with apparently such different feelings about the experience of the project, made me think. On that quiet Saturday night after the closing ceremony, the irony and the contrast between the project's aims and its accomplisments hit home. Ploughshares' intentions had been admirably idealistic: Soviet and U.S. volunteers were to demonstrate by their efforts how persons from the two economically and politically "most powerful nations" in the world, former enemies, could unite and work together. If one looked only at appearances, we had done that. In themselves, even appearances, I told myself, might be important. Still, I knew in a realistic rather than idealistic way that it had been nearly impossible to work together as a real team. With certain Soviet individuals we had achieved a good working relationship, and a fondness. With others we had failed. The good connections would last in our memories if they never had any more nourishment from letters or face-to-face meetings. Still, there were parts of our team relationships that we were all glad to see fade.

Did this mixed outcome mean that the project had not been worth planning, paying for, and doing? Never. It had been launched in faith, and part of that faith was that the outcome mattered. But so did the process—what we could learn from the very experience itself.

Since the U.S. volunteers preferred the village to Addis, we had decided to remain in camp as long as possible. Sunday morning Abebe would take us to the city in the FSO van.

As we pulled out of our grimy bed sheets at the usual hour that Sunday morning, the cooks staged a coffee ceremony at breakfast. Along with the coffee, Edil brought out a white shawl with embroidered edges to drape on Ann's head, Ethiopian-style, almost as if national dress might somehow hold Ann in Godino. Once draped, she looked like some kind of "bride of Godino." Twelve of us altogether—Ann, Noel, Jack, Beriso, Gitachew, Senbet, Asellefech, and I, joined by the cooks Edil, Jufari, Yalem Zode, and Wandosun—sat at the breakfast table cracking jokes, and singing songs—anything to cheer each other up. But in turn, people continued to fall silent. We couldn't shake the heaviness we felt. Edil and Jufari broke periodically into tears. When I sang my voice kept cracking.

Then, mysteriously, more singing began on the other side of camp. The sound came from where the path started through the demonstration field. Who was it? We listened and the chorus grew louder and moved closer until it was coming from just outside the acacia-thorn fence.

Then, above the invisible singers there appeared—bobbing up and down—a thicket of sticks. Flowers and papers attached to the stick's tops flopped about. Finally, a bevy of some twelve food-for-work workers came into view at the gate. Singing, they marched boisterously around the outside of the camp. One of the guards opened the gate wide and, bellowing their words, they trooped near to our table and formed a circle.

One of the young men removed a paper from the top of his stick and brought it to me. It said "To Ann, Gudy, Jag & Knuale. I wish you good luck to arrive in your country safely. Now good by good by good by three times. Your sincerly Kassu Gebre."

We foreigners jumped up to join their circle. Senbet came too. Up—down. Their sticks flew to the rhythm of their brassy chorus, and oleander blossoms dropped into the dust. Each U.S. volunteer's name appeared in one of the songs. Senbet tried to translate, but the whole atmosphere was too reckless and lively, and no translation reached us. We didn't need it. Humor and open hearts spoke for themselves.

The singing went on for perhaps twenty minutes. When our spirits appeared to flag and the circle didn't seem to know how to break itself, I ducked off to suggest to Abebe that he drive the van into the center of the camp to be loaded. A number of villagers had now gathered to see us off, and although I dreaded the goodbyes, I knew we could not put off saying them.

When the van was waiting outside our tents, we ran to get our gear and pack it in. A quick getaway seemed easiest, but when I turned to the gathered folk, it was clear that each of them expected an individual goodbye.

I ducked into the kitchen, where I knew Edil had disappeared. Her sobs were now so out of control that she shyed away from the company of the others. I do not recall ever having been hugged so hard. It was a long moment that she and I stood clinging to each other, recalling the pleasure of the hours we had spent trying out gestures for language, dissolving into laughter, and slinging food together in the kitchen.

On my way out to the gathering of villagers, I bumped into Beriso. Another strong hug. I remember feeling how thin his shoulders were. I found no words. How could I express the closeness I felt to Beriso and the regret at the end of that closeness? A fierce moment.

Then I moved over to our dining tables, where almost fifty people waited, having come from Gowa and Godino to wish us well. Earlier, during breakfast, Dinkenish and her ailing husband, Tadese, had come with Kenani. (Getu had expressed his adolescence in coming separately from Kenani, his mother.) Wode Bore, who had had so many husbands, was not there, but her adopted representative, Almaz, was. Sisay and Dinberie were there without Mekdes and Aserat.

I began by hugging the ones I knew well, shaking hands with the others. It felt like a huge American wedding reception line, except that I did the moving rather than the guests. Toward the end of the goodbyes, I found I wanted to hug everyone I came to so that they would not sense my affection maintained distinctions, although it did for those whom I knew better. With some folk it was most natural to kiss three times on alternating cheeks, as is the Ethiopian custom.

When at last I climbed into the front seat of the van between Abebe and Jack, I turned around and saw the medic, Negash, and his wife, Misrak, seated behind us. They would ride into Addis with Senbet, Noel, Ann, Jack, and me. Relief. I didn't have to say goodbye to everyone I cared about all at once.

Asellefech, also, was going to ride as far as Debra Zeit with us, and I asked Abebe if we had enough gas to take a bit of a side jaunt. Instead of dropping her on the street, I wanted to take her to her house so I could meet her children. Abebe said he thought there might be enough gas.

We waited sitting in the van parked in the center of camp. Everyone was seated but Ann, who was still saying long, fond goodbyes. Our friends waited with us, smiling at us through the car windows, their eyes wet. My own tears blurred the sight of them. Quick goodbyes are hard enough. Drawn-out goodbyes are worse. Finally, feeling I could bear being there no longer, I called to Ann to ask her to hurry. She obliged, cut herself short, and hoisted her slim figure into the van. The door banged shut, and the van moved over that bumpy road out of camp for the last time. I was exhausted, without words. All the way into Debra Zeit a pall of silence saved me.

As we drove through Debra Zeit, Abebe turned the motor off and on repeatedly until he stopped abruptly at the side of the road to let Asellefech out. One more blow. I was not going to get to meet Asellefech's children. He'd forgotten! Devastated, I climbed out of the front seat to hug my partner goodbye. "Don't cry, Judy," she pleaded. "Please don't cry." It was as if the only way she could keep from crying herself was to beg me not to cry. My silent tears defied her plea. Heavy as stone, I climbed back into the van, and we drove on.

When we reached Addis, the streets were subdued. The threat of civil war seemed to leave them quiet and orderly, if you can call streets scattered with pedestrians, goats, donkeys, trucks and buses orderly. Each moving being we saw seemed to be sleep-walking. Abebe drove each of us in turn to where we were staying in the city; since the house we would be house-sitting was in an outlying residential area, we were the last to be dropped off. Continuing to turn the motor on and off, he got us there with the gas he had left.

That week spent in Addis, before we could file with a great crush of passengers onto a packed plane and leave, was already a week in another world. Each morning we rose before daylight and joined our neighbors, a man and woman, who were Australian U.N. personnel, in a brisk walk. Morning in the Addis streets confronted us with a peaceful, waking world. We always took the same pot-holed street out to where vacant grassy lots with rubble lay interspersed with larger houses under construction or recently completed. The same bus driver passed us each morning with his nearly empty bus and tooted.

My favorite spot was where the road ran past a large open grassy field; there we could see a Coptic church at the far end of the field, perhaps a quarter of a mile off. Each morning as we passed that spot, the pedestrians sharing our road turned as they walked, faced the church, and genuflected.

Thursday, the night before the Soviets were due to fly out, Jack and I had arranged a gathering at a hotel for the team's final Ethiopian meal. Roba, Gitachew, Senbet, Belay, Vladik, Sergei, Olga, Ruslan, and Noel were our guests in the hotel's basement "den." Ann's parents, having heard about the threat of war, had insisted she leave Ethiopia on the first plane she could get on, so she was not with us. The food in this dark atmosphere was supposed to be, Belay told us, "the best Ethiopian food in town." Having been in the village, none of us foreigners considered ourselves connisseurs.

That evening I was impressed again at how adept Ethiopians were at eating with one hand while the other lay in their lap. We grouped ourselves around three low tables with a central tray of injeera and varying sauces on each table. Then each Ethiopian deftly tore an edge piece of the pancake-like injeera, used it to pick up a portion of one of the sauces that lay on the center of the bread, and put it into his mouth. (I, who was not accustomed to eating with my hands, was steadily tempted to use two hands to tear the injeera. But using a second hand is not polite in Ethiopia.) Everyone ate heartily, aware that this was our last meal together. But people seldom gorge themselves with Ethiopian food. The time could not be drawn out.

We finished the meal and slowly straggled upstairs and out into the street before we said goodbye. Reluctant to go, we loitered in front of the hotel. At last we could put off separating no longer. We knew we would still be seeing the Ethiopians again for goodbyes, but time had run out for the Soviets.

Ruslan and Jack approached each other. Their friendship had been so solid, so symbolic that somehow all of us paused to watch. They each said the word, "goodbye," and moved to embrace each other. But their respect for each other required some extra gesture. Suddenly Ruslan frowned. He was too short to embrace Jack face on. At the same time Gitachew, in a flash of insight, saw Ruslan's difficulty. He, who had at times seemed insensitive to other campers' needs, at that moment became impressively perceptive. He stepped forward, lifted Ruslan, as only a man as powerfully built as Gitachew could lift Ruslan, and raised him up to meet Jack face to face. The two leaders—one Soviet one American, abetted by an Ethiopian—embraced. Wonder surged from my toes to the top of my head. Thanksgiving for this moment, for the experience in Ethiopia, for the privilege of knowing our teammates, their humanity and their foibles.

Regret ran through me, also. Those three months lifted up and out of the ordinary days of my life were ended. I might return to Godino, I might see these foreign friends again, but removed from the camp's context—the tents, the latrines, the earthy work—no one would be the same, nor would I. This experience could not happen again. The three months that had ended could never be duplicated. Godino days and nights were swiftly flying backward into the past, and if I couldn't kiss them goodbye, I still had to release them with grace. I remembered a phrase from the notebooks of William Blake:

> He who binds to himself a joy
> Does the winged life destroy;
> But he who kisses the joy as it flies
> Lives in eternity's sun rise.

Epilogue

WE LEFT Ethiopia by pushing ourselves onto a plane that was going to London. At the airport the press of foreigners and Ethiopians all trying to get seats on the same plane created chaos. Our reservations had been "mislaid." We waited out a long line with countless other fretting passengers, as if we were on standby. Then in the holding lounge there was another long, uncertain wait. Our anxiety distracted us, and we did not feel the heat.

Finally our names were called and we walked out onto the tarmac, pointed to our luggage piled under the plane's tail, and entered at the back of a plane that appeared to be already full. Stuffed into a seat, separated from Jack by several rows, mixed feelings invaded me as I awaited the moment of takeoff. I tipped my head back in my seat. We were leaving the country. "It" had ended. But what were we leaving our Ethiopian friends to endure?

The confusion at the airport had caused my concern for our Ethiopian friends to mushroom. They might have to live through what could turn out to be an ongoing hell. After our week in Addis we knew that the pull-out of the Soviet Union and the new unity displayed by the rebel forces made this 1991 spring season's threat to the capital real. Who knew what chaos would soon rage through the streets of Addis? If Mengistu resisted the rebels, there would be fighting in the streets. If the rebels took over there was bound to be looting and a breakdown of law and order. Either way, chaos and violence were inevitable.

After leaving the country, the dearth of information about Ethiopia's civil war left us still more uncertain. No newspaper, no broadcast gave us significant news about what was going on.

In that state of concern, exacerbated by our newly gained ability to imagine real people and places, our comfortable life on the island seemed ironic. It wasn't that we felt guilty for the abundance in our supermarkets, our hot and cold running water, our peaceful walks on the beach; but we did feel more grateful. We were lucky enough to have been born in a privileged place.

The North American drive toward perfection struck me as a luxury. In the U.S. educational opportunities, conditions, and material well-being are such that we can aspire to strive for perfection. We demand of our fellow citizens achievement close to perfection in our search for knowledge, in our mechanical and electronic processes, in our creations. If products and processes don't emerge perfect, we look for the person or company responsible and sue them. Our Ethiopian friends don't dare aim for perfection. Their struggles are merely to cope.

In early May, Ethiopia again emerged in world news. The Jewish Ethiopians were finally being allowed to leave the country for Israel. Accounts were published of Jewish Ethiopians being jammed a thousand at once onto planes from which the seats had been stripped for transport to Israel. I visualized that crowded airport. But since we were not so concerned about the flight into Israel as the plight of our friends left in Addis, those news reports did nothing to assuage our anxiety.

On May 21, 1991, world headlines announced Mengistu's flight from Ethiopia. He was rumoured to be in Zimbabwe.

Relief that he'd removed himself from the fight didn't over-shadow our concern about the chaos he'd left behind. Slim reports emerged of fighting in Addis. Then word came that the rebels had taken over. We knew there was looting and disorder, but we heard only sparse radio reports and saw only occasional newspaper articles. I went to the library to look for newspaper reports from the larger, more interna-tionally oriented press. The rebels' first pronouncements appeared to have a remarkable lack of vindictiveness. What was really going on?

In early June we got a letter from Beriso, mailed around May 15, which reported that Asellefech and Senbet were continuing the village work and that the food-for-work folk had harvested a bumper crop from the demonstration gar-den. Camp had continued to be outside the lines of fire, and things were going well. He made no mention of anything political. However, Beriso, having been in prison, would not be expected to mention anything controversial.

On June 28 there was a gathering in Seattle of the U.S. volunteers from both the fall and winter Ploughshares teams. That night we pooled our information from sketchy accounts and letters from Ethiopia and decided to telephone Roba at his home. It would be Saturday morning in Addis.

Immediately, the telephone call went through and we were able to express our concern for all our Ethiopian team-mates. Roba assured us everyone was enduring. But, we asked, how were things going in the village?

We got shocking news! The camp had been looted. First the rebel soldiers had appeared at the camp and taken what money and medical supplies they could find. Then, when the retreating soldiers sold their guns to the villagers, they used them to raid the camp. Everything—tools, kitchen equipment, tents, camping equipment—had been stolen. They had even dismantled the corrugated iron buildings and carried off the sheets of iron to use in other places. As a final ironic gesture, the farmers had turned their cattle into the demonstration field to pick at the leavings after the harvest.

We hung up the phone feeling devastated. We refused to believe that the same villagers with whom we had worked had destroyed our camp, but it had been completely destroyed.

Roba had confirmed our fears. That early June in Ethiopia had been a time of terrible chaos, a time when law and order were nonexistent, and men had license to turn to angry, violent acts in order to survive. FSO was not alone. Mobs had robbed and looted other relief projects as well. As for the new government the rebels were forming, Roba said Ethiopians were watching and waiting for a meeting that would take place the following Monday, July 1. The rebels had called leaders of many parties together to try to form a new, more democratic government. Roba also told us that he and the Chairman of the FSO Board were coming to the U.S in August (we guessed they were coming to raise funds for FSO).

In a letter written June 26, Beriso said:

Godino is really not Godino you know, this time. Everything has been taken (robbed) by the farmers as well as food-for-work workers. No activity in Godino for the time being. We have reported to Debre Zeit new government officials, and they are trying to collect some items taken by forming a committee, and I wonder how we can reorganize Godino again since the farmers and workers we were helping robbed us.

Judy and Jack, the new government is settling the condition and the country from day to day, and there will be meeting which will be held in Addis Ababa on July 1 for transition government, and I hope good things will come out of this.

Browns, I hope you have herd [sic] yesterday's President Mengistu Haile Mariame became farmer in one of the African Country. I wonder if he knows double dig and how to make composting. As far as I know he knows only fighting and killing as well as putting people in prison.

At least now Beriso felt free to write something openly critical of Mengistu!

In September, Roba came to Seattle with Kindeya Hailu and brought word of a major change for FSO. After the looting, the FSO Board searched its organizational soul. Were they going to muster forgiveness and continue working with the same villages that had turned on their camp and looted it?

Yes. FSO leaders felt called upon to start the work again. They would attempt to raise the funds to return to the Godino project with a new name and a new vision. Family Service Organization would become Vision of Hope (VOH). Its new thrust was more openly Christian and it had a new emphasis: to empower the people with whom it worked to become new, whole persons. VOH cared about helping people become more self-sufficient, but they also cared about their lives as whole persons, which implied concern for their spiritual lives.

I heard of Vision of Hope's new aims with relief. I had been to Ethiopia. I had seen that many Ethiopians endure poverty without really knowing they are poor. I had been charmed by the simplicity with which they take to life in the village, and I had delighted in their humor. I had felt their anguish at the war and the civil unrest they were having to endure, and I cared. I wanted caring agricultural work to go on with the people we had worked with, not because I was certain it would have lasting results, but because I was certain it was good work.

To say it was good work was in no way to say it was "perfect" work. I was now convinced that Ethiopians lacked sophistication when it came to fashioning an agricultural project, honing the process in which they worked, and operating in such a way as to bring out the best energy and creativity of those participating in the effort. Particularly in assigning the leadership and work of our camp, they had made what I perceived as errors. But having been there to see the conditions under which they worked, how could I demand perfection of an Ethiopian organization? I knew the background and shoe-string nature of the effort. What was important was that they made the effort and the spirit in which it was made. Those villagers who had experienced its goodness were bound to remember it significantly.

While Roba and his board chairman, Kindeya, were still in Seattle, a brief note, written September 5, came from Belay in Addis Ababa:

> I am very much pleased to inform you that we have started Godino project again. As I have written you last time, I have been going around Embassies and Big NGOs pleading to rehabilitate Godino. Thanks God, German Embassy has allocated 2,000 DM and CRDA has donated us 173MT grain. Now we are working on compost since it is high time for the availability of green materials in the surroundings as it rains.

Later we learned that because there was no way to pay so many food-for-work workers, the land in the camp's double-dug demonstration plots was parceled out for use by "contact farmers" willing to restore and work it. The plan conceived by Beriso, Asellefech, and Senbet was to let twenty contact farmers work the land for a growing season and then rotate to twenty others. These three, as VOH staff persons, would act as educators and aids. Another good idea had emerged in Godino; but for some reason we didn't understand, the directors of VOH in the Addis office were only lukewarm about that idea.

In February of 1992, Roba, his wife, daughter and brother-in-law arrived in Seattle, and Roba was given an office to use in one of Seattle's evangelically oriented churches. They rented a comfortable apartment in a section of the city near the airport where rents were slightly less high. We lent him our car to use to get a driver's license, and he passed the driver's test with no trouble. The family found a comfortable used van to buy (it was about two years old) for $4,000.

I helped Roba put out a newsletter about VOH's operations in Ethiopia and the U.S. In working with him on the newsletter it became clear that his chief interest in Ethiopia at that time was not the Godino project. A new cause had captured his main interest: he described a group of twenty-five young orphans whom VOH had befriended when they were turned out of their Coptic Orthodox Christian orphanage because they had been converted from Coptic Christianity and become Evangelical Christians. VOH had taken these orphans off the streets of Addis, set up a place for them to live, and attempted to get them all in school. In the newsletter, Roba printed pictures of each of these young students, described their new living situation, and lauded their courage in sticking to their new-found faith in the face of persecution from their former care-givers. He urged VOH supporters to adopt an orphan. There was little appeal for funds to continue any development work in Ethiopia, though there were reports of the work of various projects.

By the late spring of 1992, VOH had laid Asellefech off of the Godino project. She wrote us that she had begged Kindeya to let her continue working in Godino and be paid merely with food-for-work grain and oil. Instead, she said, he sold the grain and oil. In May of 1992 Belay and his new wife appeared in Seattle on their way to do agricultural development work in Bangladesh with another U.S.-based organization, Land and Water Resources International. His report was that things were not going well in the Ethiopian office of VOH. At that time we were speaking continuously with Beriso by telephone about his coming to the U.S. to study, and he informed us that the organizations, such as the German Embassy and CARE, which had formerly supported the Godino project were beginning to question VOH's purposes.

In private conversations with Roba, I tried to get a straight story from him as to where the funds that were supporting him in the U.S. were coming from and why development workers in Godino were being laid off. I got no answer that satisfied me. Instead, I began to wonder if Roba was using his Evangelical zeal to justify his misuse of funds in the U.S. I wrote Roba a letter about my concern and he told me on the telephone that I didn't know what I was talking about.

In September of 1992 Roba closed the Seattle VOH office and informed VOH friends that he would pursue ministerial studies at Oral Roberts University in Tulsa, Oklahoma. Beriso arrived in early November of 1992 to live with our family and other U.S. friends and pursue studies at Seattle Central Community College. He confirmed our fears that VOH was no longer interested in development work in Ethiopia. Kindeya had been sending evangelists to Godino rather than agricultural workers. VOH had continued to sell the grain and oil given to them to pay agricultural workers, and Beriso did not know where those funds were being used.

We were sad when we heard this news. The change of motivation and breakdown of development work seemed to us to be a great loss to Ethiopia. This altered direction, however, could never wipe out the initial good motives and push for development work that had led to the founding of Family Service Organization and kept it going initially. Though discontinued, its early work would always stand as pioneering. Ethiopians had founded their own organization aiming to help other Ethiopians to be more self-reliant.